A FIELD OF SCARLET POPPIES

ALSO BY JENNIFER DAWSON

The Ha-Ha
Fowler's Snare
The Cold Country
Strawberry Boy
The Queen of Trent (with Elizabeth Mitchell)
Hospital Wedding (stories)

A FIELD OF SCARLET POPPIES

JENNIFER DAWSON

QUARTET BOOKS
LONDON MELBOURNE NEW YORK

First published by Quartet Books Limited 1979
A member of the Namara Group
27 Goodge Street, London W1P 1FD

Copyright © 1979 by Jennifer Dawson

ISBN 0 7043 2189 0

Typesetting by Gavin Martin Limited

Printed in Great Britain by offset lithography by
Billing & Sons Ltd, Guildford, London and Worcester

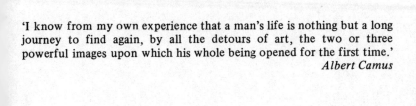

'I know from my own experience that a man's life is nothing but a long journey to find again, by all the detours of art, the two or three powerful images upon which his whole being opened for the first time.'

Albert Camus

A FIELD OF SCARLET POPPIES

CHAPTER 1

A pregnant day in mid May when every green thing in the street seemed about to burst its boundaries.

'I think I convinced them I was the one for the job' Thelma had told you when she got in from the interview last night. 'We had an interesting talk about Virginia Woolf and the Spanish Civil War. The interview went well, I think. I'm sure' she had flung her arms round your neck, 'that at last I've found a really worthwhile job where I can be doing something useful at last in the neighbourhood. Do you follow me? Or am I talking absolute rot? Do you get my drift? And I liked all the people in the library and felt that I should soon have friends round here after all. It's so much easier to make friends when you are all working together towards some specific goal. And we got into a long discussion about music and I told them about you being a cellist in a quartet. And I told them about my flute. Oh Will,' she flung her arms round you again, 'at last I think I've found my feet. I'm putting down roots here after all these years. And when I got on to the bus after the interview, I felt at one with all the women cleaners and packers and oversewers coming home from work. I too have got honest work now, if you see my drift.'

But the letter turning down her application for an assistant librarian's job must have been written as soon as she left the interview because it had arrived next day at breakfast. When you went to the refrigerator to get out some milk you saw that two bottles of barley wine had gone and that Thelma's speech was slurred.

1

'You've been drinking already' you smelt her breath. Tears ran down her cheeks. She had tipped the barley wine over the table and was mopping it up with a J-cloth and squeezing it back into the glass then drinking the squeezings, as she wept.

'That's the last time I shall try to get a job. Does one try again? Do you get my meaning? Am I making myself plain?'

She wore an onyx ring you had given her years ago, but it had always been too big and kept slipping round to the palm side of her hand and she would try to prop it in its place on the front of her finger with two pieces of matchstick which she jammed on the inside of her finger. But they kept falling out so that the flat was littered with broken matchsticks. When you saw them lying on the table or the floor you would instantly hear her voice:

'If you see my meaning . . . If you get my drift . . . If I'm not talking absolute tosh. Am I on your beam? Are we in "sync" today?'

'But why do you want a job?' You picked up a broken matchstick. 'I'd give anything to have six months off to try and get over this drought. Six months to practise the strange harsh broken John Wersby quartet before we perform it at Cambridge. Why don't you go down to Dorset for a few days? I wish I had a month to go down there and master the quartet instead of staying here and rehearsing it so hurriedly and wretchedly without any real understanding of what he had in mind and why he died. Some memorial concert in Cambridge. The manuscript copies are so impossibly illegible that we never really know if we are playing what he intended.'

'And how did he die?'

'Just did himself in. No one knows why. Left a house full of blacks. I wish I didn't have to play anything for six months. Just go underground and then perhaps my obsession would come back.'

'You wouldn't like it for long' Thelma wept again. 'Oh what shall I do?'

'Drink some black coffee first and instead of going round to the off-license when I've gone out, go and visit a friend.'

'You know I have no friends.'

'A lot of people ask after you. Nancy for example.'

2

'Only out of politeness. Nancy is always so absorbed in the quartet. She has no time for lesser women.'

'And George asks after you.'

'That is just guilt because he avoids me so much.' She went to her bag and pulled out her cigarettes with stiff, jerky movements, every movement planned, willed and executed carefully. She had learned to control herself when she was tight.

'Perhaps Julius will drop in for lunch then.'

'My life would be unendurable without Julius popping in from time to time. I only feel real when I'm with him. He's the only member of the quartet who brings me alive.'

'Sounds like an advertisement for Fanta or Fresca or Seven-up. What about Mrs Stein? Why don't you invite her again?'

Mrs Stein was Thelma's flute teacher. Thelma had asked her several times to come to lunch and bring her flute with her so that they could play some duets. Mrs Stein came once and without her flute; stuck her fork into a leaf of wet pallid cabbage and tore a piece off and chewed. Thelma had chopped red cabbage and plunged it into boiling water and watched the red streaming out and the cabbage become white and flaccid. 'How funny' she had said, 'I've been married all these years and I never knew red cabbage did that.'

Mrs Stein had chewed. The pâté was secreting yellow fat at its edges. Mrs Stein eased it gently to the side of her plate and sipped water.

'That is why I enjoy my flute lessons so much' Thelma was saying. Her words were slurred. She had been drinking again in the kitchen, gulping down barley wines as she changed the plates. You went out and found an empty bottle stuffed inside a cornflakes packet under the sink.

'. . . because I want to grasp things of eternal value' Thelma was saying when you got back. 'There is so much chaos and misery in the world. The Bomb. Vietnam. Do you get my meaning? Art seems to lift emotion out of squalor and into beauty if you see my drift . . .' Thelma had long dark hair and pale green eyes and a hooked nose and a pointed chin . . . a face waiting for mining; waiting for

3

excavation; extraction.

'Do you think along these lines at all?' Mrs Stein nodded slightly and perched a radish on her fork and let it splash into the pool of cabbage water on her plate.

'Do you have a heavy week's teaching?'

'I do a little teaching during the week but I have a family.'

'And what do you enjoy teaching most? Which composer?'

'It depends on who my pupils are.' Mrs Stein balanced the dripping radish on her fork again and tried to get it into her mouth. There was silence into which Thelma blurted:

'Which do you like best? Which composer do you feel most for? I mean' she added when she saw how childish the question was — she always became like a child when she most hoped for a passionate conversation about music or Vietnam or the Bomb — 'do you find Mahler a great composer?' she asked in her desperate hunger.

Mrs Stein pushed the radish to one side of her plate: 'I admire the "Song of the Earth" very much but my heart is not there.'

'Where is your heart then? Which composer gives you the greatest sense of eternity?' Mrs Stein extracted the stub end of a cigarette from her potato and pushed it to the side of her plate, drew out her handkerchief and coughed:

'I am a musician. I find that many roads lead the same way.'

'And do you enjoy your teaching? Or is it a chore at the end of a busy day?'

'I am always grateful if I can help musicians to realise a little of their potential.' She shook the slice of pâté that had become soaked in the plate's wet. You could see her neat ox-blood boots crossing and recrossing under the table. And Thelma had splashes of paint on her glasses. She had had them there since she distempered a bedroom wall three months ago.

'I suppose you have some very talented young pupils?'

'A lot of young people have talent. Sixteen is the testing time I find.'

'How many children have you got?'

'Three.'

4

'And do they all play as well?'

'The eldest wants to be an engineer.' Mrs Stein took a spoonful out of the stiff pink sweet mixture Thelma had made. It made a sucking sound as it clicked away from the hard pink pad on her plate. 'I don't believe in children necessarily following their parents' vocations. Mine are all different from me.' The spoonful of pink was poised at her mouth. Then it fell back into her dish. 'Excuse me.'

'I had hoped you would bring your flute so that we could play the Loeillet' Mrs Stein gave a faint smile. Thelma cleared the plates and went out. You could hear her opening another barley wine and gulping it back before she came back in and laid six cream crackers and three triangles of processed cheese on the table.

'A most satisfactory meal' Mrs Stein pushed her cheese plate away. 'But really I am not used to eating so much at lunchtime.'

'It must be a wonderful life being so close to great lives and Plato's eternal Forms. When I feel that life is pointless I always console myself with the thought of my philosophy class or our Wednesday wind classes. I remember the first time I came, you were doing the Schubert "Octet".'

'Yes, we had some good musicians in those days. I expect you are too busy for very much practice.'

'Two hours most days, and those are the richest part of the day. Do you get my meaning? Am I making myself plain?'

Mrs Stein acknowledged the question by lowering her head and sipping her water.

Thelma's face was flushed: 'If only I could play the flute like you.'

'Thank you. And now I must say goodbye and thank you both . . .'

'Why didn't you say anything?' Thelma asked angrily when she had gone, and now you were asking stupidly:

'So why don't you invite Mrs Stein again?'

'The professional woman is always bored by her less successful sisters. She had no time for me. I wanted to talk about Plato's Forms in relation to music. Do you get my meaning? Or am I talking the most utter rot?'

'Try to stop saying that.'

'Saying what?'

' "Do you get my meaning? . . . Am I making myself plain?" '

Thelma put her hand to her mouth. Matchstick ends fell on to the table.

'Well, I must know. I can't live in suspense the whole time wondering if I am talking rot or not. I suppose the children are ashamed of me.'

The phone went. She picked up the receiver.

'Is that Thea?' a young child's breathy voice came down the line.

'Nearly right. It's Thelma.'

'Are you young?'

'No I'm not. I'm mid-fortyish.'

'Then fuck off the line you silly old bitch.' She put the receiver down and went to the fridge for another barley wine.

'That might have been Andrew.'

'If you will put on that girlish flirtatious manner. You invited that. Now come and have some black coffee and get sober.'

Andrew, your youngest, when he was home for the school holidays, would drift in when Thelma was tuning her flute.

'That's not an A.' He hummed an A. 'Don't you see? You're miles away. Listen' he would hum again.

'That might have been Andrew on the phone' Thelma repeated. 'You should have married a professional woman like Nancy instead of an inarticulate one who was trained for nothing but making herself pleasing to men and not even succeeding in that. One doesn't want to put all one's eggs in one basket. That's why I go to my classes. To try and understand. And yet I'm nothing. My life took place one day when I was living with my father and he turned aside to sneeze. Tishoo. That's all. Everything. For ever. That's why I drink. But if I had worthwhile work to do . . .'

'You could go and visit old Miss Hasten this morning. And the Citizens' Advice Bureau is always crying out for volunteers.'

'And the "Artificial Limbs Centre" requires a canteen

helper. And the "Central Foster Bible Trust" seeks a reliable secretary . . . Ring Julie if you are the girl for the job . . .' She dropped cigarette ash into the salt cellar. 'Sorry' she apologised, and dropped it into a little Chinese basket full of reels of cotton and blew on them. You fetched an ashtray.

'If you had a woman friend' you said gently, 'she would weep every time she smelt your breath and saw you were tight.'

'Sorry.'

'But I'm glad you are coming to Cambridge with us next week. Why don't you come with us more often now that the children are off your hands?'

'Sitting round in dark halls while you rehearse. Sitting about in hotels while you perform. And when I do come, you all seem so . . . so together. I feel as though I'm the only one who isn't treated as a real person. And I'm so tired of hearing the Razumovskys' and your post-mortems. And I'm tired of being Will Parrish's wife. A tiresome appendage like a suitcase you've got to lug around with you. I must have my own friends and a worthwhile job for myself.'

'I've never wanted you to feel obliged to prove yourself in that way. You have proved yourself to me by bringing up two children and giving them the warmth and love that they need. And me. I need it when I come in frustrated and exhausted. You keep me in touch with a kinder and less competitive kind of life. I don't want to come home to a wife who has joined the rat-race.'

'No. You want a wife who makes herself indispensable to you like a pair of bedroom slippers or an electric blanket.'

'Well, that is how our society used to be organised and you are not equipped, thank God, to do anything else. Professional women, with all respect to Nancy, depress me. They usually seem to get things so wrong.'

'Women on the whole haven't been convinced yet that they can be other than a wife and a mother or a filing clerk or a receptionist. And that's the fault of men like you.'

'Well what about that job that you had at the Royal Free?'

'Dealing out fags and deodorants and toothpastes.'

'And you had that job on the geriatric ward.'

7

'Helping senile old ladies with their bingo cards. Helping them make those hideous plastic ashtrays that lie about in their thousands in geriatric wards because no one wants to buy them.'

Or she would go round the neighbours in the block offering herself as a baby-sitter: 'I'm always here. We don't go out much.'

'You would offer yourself as a grave-digger to Camden Borough Council if they would have you.' And there was that job in the Family Planning Clinic. Thelma had got there tight though and had doled out Eugynon 30 instead of 50. And Microgynon instead of Ovranyl.

'Well, so what is there for me?'

'You have a lofty view of your own capacities. Perhaps that was why they turned you down at the library yesterday.'

'One only wants life to be not quite so pointless.'

'You have your home visiting.'

'Yes, and how ashamed I am taking them a packet of tea and a tangerine at Christmas and a small bunch of primroses at Easter when what they need is companionship all day and square meals and not being shut up in those lonely tower blocks.'

'We must do what we can. And I once needed you as you were. Perhaps we should move though.'

'Where to?'

'Out of Central London. Out of Holborn. Into some suburb where you would meet people of your own class.'

'I hate our class. I hate my voice. They laugh at me in Exmouth Market and imitate my accent.'

'All the more reason why we should move.'

'In Kensington or Hampstead I should still be just your wife. I shall stand about at the party at Cambridge next week as your wife. Answering questions about you and whether the children play too. Last time we went to a party all the women kept talking about their husbands. How many men keep referring to their wives like that?'

'I often mention you in conversations.'

'What do you say?'

'I tell people what a good wife and mother you are.'

8

'Exactly, Will. Exactly.'

'In fact I find most women rather boring.'

'You don't help them much by asking after the "Bonnie Babes". And the quartet, they patronise me. They come up to me and try to be nice and say: "I did so much enjoy that conversation I had with you about Sartre last week. A most engaged and committed discussion. The best serious talk I have had for a long time".' Thelma burst into laughter.

'If people are friendly to you at parties you accuse them of being patronising and insincere. If they don't happen to talk to you, you accuse them of ostracising you. But promise me you will try to keep off Vietnam and the Spanish Civil War in Cambridge next week. There will be people there who will be much better informed than you about non-alignment politics in the thirties.'

'That's the only time I feel real.'

'It's become your cards of identity.'

You could hear her there at the party as soon as she had got a bit tight, holding forth to her hostess:

'They all talked about non-intervention in Spain, but as early as the spring of 1936 Sanjurjo was with Hitler in Berlin making arrangements for the shipping of armaments to the Fascist insurgents. Before the war had even begun.'

'I'm afraid I'm really one of the thousands of "Don't knows" as far as Spain is concerned' her hostess would reply. 'Do you play as well?'

'The flute. But not very well. Of course we should have invaded Spain in 1945. The Republicans were all expecting it. It was a crime not to. But the Americans wouldn't have it. Roosevelt had made some agreement with Spain much earlier. Do you get my meaning? Am I making myself clear?'

'Yes. Of course. But I love Spain. We go there nearly every year. Which part do you know?'

'None. I shall never go there till Franco is dead and Fascism buried.'

'I admire your integrity. But we do love the sunshine and the cities and the people. They seem to be quite happy under the régime.'

'The ones who don't happen to be Republicans and

9

Socialists may be.'

'Come and meet Mrs Neary.'

And so the party would go on.

'If I had been adult during the Spanish Civil War . . .' Thelma had begun.

'There would never have been a Fascist victory' you interrupted brutally. 'Try to keep off the subject of Spain and Vietnam. When we're in Cambridge' you begged her.

'What makes you think I want to come to Cambridge?' She started to clear the breakfast things away. 'Why don't we ever invite anyone here as we used to during C.N.D. and Vietnam?'

'You know why.'

When you did invite anyone in for a meal Thelma would slip off to the off-licence and come back with Cyprus sherry which she hid in the box-room.

'What are you doing in there?' you would call.

'Just tidying up. Clearing away some of the children's mess.'

And when the guests came she would stagger in talking about Guernica or Hiroshima or the bombing of Hanoi. And now the N.L.F. victory.

'You vulgarise and trivialise all serious subjects when you are tight. And you've no idea how pathetic you look always clutching that packet of cigarettes and those matches. It sickens me to see you making this gross transformation of yourself and your subject. Your speech slurred. Your politics insincere. Your face contorted and your accent dragged through half a dozen diphthongs in one word. Why do you go away from me like this? Why do you want to concuss yourself? You aren't a navvy on a building site. The man in the off-licence or the pub can afford to treat you as an alcoholic and pretend with a wink that this is your first drink of the day and pass you over the booze. But I have to live with you and treat you as a human being . . . as a human being who makes statements that are true or false, true or insincere. And when I see that they are inauthentic, little by little my love withdraws as though its roots had hit something hard and acid in the soil and you become an alcoholic "thing" whose statements about Spain or Vietnam or what you were doing in the box-room all have to be taken with a

10

pinch of salt. Not the person I once knew and loved.'

Thelma went into the kitchen and ran the tap, but even above its loud thundering into the plastic basin in the sink, you could hear her opening another barley wine.

'Where have you been?' you asked when she came back.

'Just to see that I hadn't left the gas-tap on.' She gave a slight belch and started to clear the breakfast things.

'Why do you have to go away from me like this?'

'Because I feel so starved for honest work and human companionship. But why do I have to keep reminding you, if you get my meaning . . . if you see my drift?'

'Try to stop saying "If you get my meaning . . . if you see my drift". It's only a way of disguising your anger and trying to sound moderate and reasonable.'

'I am moderate and reasonable.'

'Your anger is terrible. You drink to drown it.'

'I drink because you and the children are always snubbing me and cutting me down to size. That's why I always end "If you see my drift".'

'I love you and the children love you too.'

'They despise me. You take recordings of their conversation and their playing, and they turn on me:

' "Go away! You wouldn't understand this. And your conversation is boring and you are getting fat and your hair falls out." The children have started copying you.'

'You are talking perfect rot' Andrew would tell her, it was true. And Martin would add:

'Try and keep your bird-brain on the matter in hand.'

Once in a heat wave when she had been sitting on the balcony all week in the sun and her arms had started to peel, Andrew had sat at the supper table staring at the ribbons of transparent peeling skin clinging off her arms and turning to grey balls of dirty pith where she had rubbed them. He had sat there without eating his supper. Then he had got up:

'Do you mind putting on a cardigan or something? Your arms are putting me off my food.'

'You have taught them to despise me' she accused you. 'If only we had sent them to local schools. They would have been closer to me now and I would have got to know other

11

mothers and have friends now.'

'Pressers and needlehands and blockmakers' wives. You wouldn't be getting much joy out of them.'

'You are growing more and more anti-working-class. You used not to be during C.N.D.'

'I get on all right with my fellow-men.' Thelma drank again. This time openly.

'Do you want to end up on the "meths" and the surgical spirit?' The wind lifted the leaves outside in the churchyard gardens gently like a lapping tide. Fountains of green sprang up among the grey brick wholesalers' shops of the Gray's Inn Road. Thelma started to carry the breakfast things into the kitchen with slow and careful and consciously controlled movement. 'Do you want to end up on the "Jack"?' you cried after her, 'sitting round the fire on the bomb-site in the East End, the fire that never goes out? The fire that is fed twenty-four hours a day by wood from demolition sites, keeping your feet near the blaze in winter because only last week one of the alcoholics got frostbite and had to have seven toes off and was out of hospital on crutches before they had discharged him and before he could walk again, hobbling swiftly back to the fire that never goes out and the chemist nearby that never closes, the chemist where you tap on the window and a head appears upstairs and lowers a basket into which you put your thirty pence. And down comes the basket with the "meths" or the "Surge". Do you want to end on the "Jack"? In the East End, selling your winter coat in February to get the last ten pence you need for the "Jack"? Putting it on the scales though the weather is bitter and getting your ten pence so that you can rap on the chemist's windows? Don't you think you ought to go back to your Alcoholics Anonymous group? Try it again.'

'Oh they are as smug as a Revivalist meeting in a canvas cathedral' Thelma replied unmoved. 'Only instead of being washed clean in the Blood of the Lamb they find their grace through the "Higher Power" and through the wonderful fellowship of A.A. I got no fellowship there. Only a lot of emotional men who were once the worst of sinners. In the end I felt unworthy of them like a nun during Holy Week

when all the other members of the community are living on
boiled potatoes and hot water and she sneaks out into the
kitchen when they are all at Compline and gets cold toast
from the garbage can and spreads it with bright sweet red jam
and makes another meal before they all come out.'

'Most women drink because they have lost their husbands.
You drink because you have one. I saved you from becoming
an old maid when you were your father's secretary booking
up his concerts for him when he was so deaf with tinnitus
that he could no longer play in tune. You were his secretary
when he was forced to retire because he couldn't play in tune
and came to recitals with a deaf-aid. I saved you from
spinsterhood and the typists' pool.'

Thelma could have replied: 'And I saved you from homo-
sexuality when you were living with John Wersby. It was I
who enabled you to become heterosexual and have children
whom you love. So there's no need for you to accuse me of
being a mere old maid whom you were sorry for. It was you
who needed me.'

She could have said it but she didn't. Instead she went to
the front door and wrote a note for the milkman: 'No music
today thank you'. Then she went into the bathroom and ran
the taps and you regretted your cruelty and banged on the
bathroom door:

'I'm sorry, Thelma. Open up. I want to say . . . I want to
take back what I said and say that I love you even when you
do get tight. That was a spiteful thing of me to say and
totally untrue. Turn the tap off!' You shouted louder over
the running water and banged on the door again: 'Open up
please!'

She turned the taps off. She came and stood naked in the
door of the bathroom.

'How much does it cost us each week, your drinking? Not
too much. Not too bad. We can afford that. Only I want you.
I need you. And you can't help me when you're tight. I need
you to help me get rid of this dryness. Only I can never talk
about it with you when you are tight. It's not the money.
That's nothing. It's that you go away from me when I most
need you. When I feel at my most arid and parched and void.

13

Oh help me. You must help me. We will try harder. We'll try to begin again. "And from this day my life shall date".'

She stood there naked against you. You kissed her wet arms and neck and cheeks. 'I must go now. We are starting at ten this morning.' You packed your cello and your music case. You hugged her again and let her wet hair drop on your neck. 'My honey-bun. I wish I were a warm loving man, a patient man instead of an irritable one. There must be some men who would be authentically sympathetic. Men who are stable enough and well-enough founded in themselves to give you loving support when you have these cravings and feelings of loneliness. Instead I give you nothing but irritation and boredom. I thought that when we got married ours would be an equal partnership, but now I have an invalid to nurse, and that is not equality. If you stopped drinking then we might have the more equal relationship you are always talking about.'

'I will try harder' she clung to your tweed jacket.

'And please don't drink before we go to Julius's at Thorley tomorrow. You know how well you get on together when you are sober and how much he likes you.'

'I'll do my best I promise you. Will you be in to lunch?'

'No we must work right through if we are to master the John Wersby quartet. We'll have lunch at the Conca D'Oro. I feel I must cling to the quartet if I am ever to be rid of this void and this drought.'

'We'll get you through it' she kissed you. 'I won't drink any more today and I won't mention Vietnam or Spain.'

You kissed her mouth: 'You said in your sleep last night: "The waves are waving at me and I am waving back".'

'I dreamed I was in a pub with Julius and he said "The world is in the hands of the bees".'

'Perhaps he was right. It certainly isn't in our hands. I dreamed that the quartet was dancing but when I spoke to them they were suddenly still and sand dribbled out of their mouths, sawdust it was perhaps, or something that goes hard like plaster of Paris. Perhaps today when we start to practise Beethoven's Opus 130, the Holy Paraclete will come. At last it will come.'

14

Then you went out. Out into the busy traffic-fumed Gray's Inn Road and into the churchyard gardens beside the Royal Free Hospital. You were early for the rehearsal and you thought you would sit there for a moment and recover yourself. You sat down and inhaled the smell of hyacinths and watched the blackbirds showering themselves with blossom, and the huge octopus roots of the great flowering chestnut tree, its leaves straining downwards, its flowers yearning upwards, straining from the dry earth to the sky. 'I wonder' you thought, 'if Thelma stopped drinking . . . if Thelma were happy again . . . if Thelma became once more the person I loved when I first met her during C.N.D. . . . I wonder if I no longer had the role of nurse . . . if things were beautiful again . . . I wonder if my own problem would grow larger . . . if the drought would expand and some horrible void open . . . or if I should just go mad and think I was Casals, or start rhyming everything the quartet said . . .' You were to get an answer sooner than you expected.

The birds were singing bell-like through the trees. The grass was still very wet. The dew still so heavy and silver that it reminded you of being very young again and very near the ground with its early morning smells of wood and grass and twigs. You would take a day off as soon as the Cambridge concert was over, you thought innocently. You would take a train down to Sussex and get off at the high wooden railway platform-halt standing on the marshes a couple of miles from the village where you had once lived as a child.

CHAPTER II

Thelma was sober next morning as you set off for Julius's cottage at Thorley. She had drunk nothing and seemed elated at the thought of the visit and looked good in her long Indian dress and her long hair loose.

The day began cheerfully enough. You kissed her after breakfast as she was combing her hair: 'Be good today. Don't go away from me.'

'I won't.'

She dusted some black soot from the windowsill and watched it float back and settle again. She got out the furniture polish and smeared it over the greasy marks on the table and spread a piece of the *Morning Star* over the floor and tipped chicken bones and cigarette ash from last night's supper into it. She bundled the paper up. The chicken bones and dead matches burst through the thin paper bundle and spilled over the floor. She scooped them up and thrust them into an empty fruit-juice tin, got a cloth and wiped it over the cigarette ash that still lay on the lino and rinsed it in the washing up water. The ash floated on top. She tipped the dirty dishes into the bowl and turned a jet of water over them. The jet hit a spoon and spurted upwards at her, drenching her neck and her face.

'Bad luck.' You both laughed.

'Now why did it have to go and do that?' She shook water off her face and you got a towel and wiped it. You kissed her as you wiped her face and eyes. She put on some rubber gloves and jammed her hands into the washing-up basin. A fork pierced the gloves and hung there dangling from her thumb. The gloves were swollen at the fingertips, loose and flabby and full of water.

'Why doesn't the material world obey me today?' she cried.

'Probably because you don't love it enough. But I should hate it if you did. Imagine having to take my outdoor shoes off when I came in and you insisting on hoovering inside my cello.'

You went to get the car out. When you came back the bathwater was running out. There was a rim of grey scum round its sides. You rubbed it with Ajax while Thelma got dressed. As she stood naked in front of the bathroom mirror you saw her again happily. Hands with fingers at the ends, all independent, all doing different things. Toes all working independently as she stood first on one foot then on the other putting her stockings on. Then you looked at her large green eyes; like lock-gates you thought, opening and shutting miraculously to let in or hold out great tracts of the unknown. Worlds dismissed at a touch when she closed her lids. Eyes that saw what was new and what was familiar and knew the difference. Eyes that recognised the same things again and again without having to start from square one each time. Eyes shutting out everything there was. You stood there with your arm round her naked body:

'You look so attractive when you are sober.'

'One glass of sherry at Julius's. That's all. I promise you.'

You drove out of central London, through the grey suburbs of Croydon and the red brick of commuterland. And then suddenly you were out among the bright green fields that you had longed for last week as you rehearsed.

'Good?' you asked. Thelma nodded.

But when you got down to Julius's, he was in one of his worst moods — being young.

'Hi!' He pushed back his long lanky black hair that hung down to his chest. He had a wild, pagan, delinquent look. 'My hair won't grow beyond my nipples' he pushed it back from his eyes. 'But Thelma's will.' He kissed her. 'Sexual inequality. Report it. Discrimination!'

His feet and chest were bare and he had tied up his dirty

17

jeans with his old school tie. He must have apologised about you to Annick, the young French girl with blonde hair and dark bulging eyes. She wore a cheesecloth blouse and jeans torn off below the knee. She spoke good English with only a slight lift at the ends of her words to indicate she wasn't English. Julius must have apologised to her for forcing her to meet such dull heavy people because he put on a mock courteous expression when he spoke as though he had to remind her all the time that he was enduring you with his tongue in his cheek. It was as if everything he said were designed to show that your relationship with him was only slight and casual and faintly ridiculous.

'Sorry we are late' you said when you arrived.

'Late?' he replied sitting on his cottage doorstep and cleaning his thick yellow toenails. 'What are "early" and "late" but bourgeois concepts?' Annick tittered. Thelma laughed. You went inside and sat down and picked a book out of his shelf.

'The trouble with that kind of anti-Soviet stuff' Julius watched you reading, 'is that as soon as you begin to criticise Soviet Russia you find yourself in such odious company. Birchers and floggers and the National Front. Have some nuts' he passed a bowl round. The nuts tasted of curry.

'Are these from India?' you asked.

'Oh really memsahib, yes they are. Do you mind wog nuts? You won't get V.D. from them if that's what you're afraid of.' There was a laugh from Thelma and Annick. Then there was silence. Julius could never stand this.

'I've come to the conclusion' he munched, 'that the child rapist is really trying to destroy the innocent child within himself. Out of fear for his threatened adulthood. When you shoot a tiger' he pulled some coins from his pocket and put them in a pile on his sitting-room floor sitting cross-legged beside them and absent-mindedly spitting on them and polishing them. 'When you shoot a tiger you are really trying to shoot the savage Id within yourself. That is what you are really afraid of.'

'But a tiger has sharp teeth and claws' Annick protested. 'You are first of all afraid of them because of your physical existence.'

'One is never simply afraid of teeth and claws' Julius munched. 'One is really only afraid of whatever it is in one's self that teeth and claws only represent.'

'I'd like to see you in a jungle then' Annick muttered. 'I'd have such pleasure sitting in my landrover with a gun and telling you as the tiger drew near that there was no need for you to try and escape because you can never escape from yourself. So stay and be torn to pieces while you conquer the death instinct in yourself. You will take that with you however fast you run.'

'Julius means hunting. Fox hunting' Thelma said, cheerfully sipping at her first glass of sherry.

'Yes, I do. I go out with an aerosol spray in front of the hounds when they come near here.'

'What do you do about fire precautions with all this thatch?' you heard yourself ask, trying to join in; trying to love your fellow men.

'Oh memsahib I don't worry. Perhaps I should rip it all off and have concrete tiles put on. Fire-hazards' he walked over his table-top. 'Pretty rigorous I imagine in your bourgeois mansions. Your Edwardian mansions. Do you mind that there is no lift here? You'll have to hoof it I'm afraid to the lats.' A great spider walked across the ceiling.

'That reminds me of some spider crabs I saw the other day' you said. 'I stopped in Chapel Market for about ten minutes at a stall loaded with huge grey lobsters and spider crabs. They were still alive and would suddenly jerk out a feeler at me trying to catch my attention; trying to haul themselves to the top of the pile. Then something bright inside the head would twitch, a winking inner eye flashing on and off despairingly in that dark interior.'

'I've always said killing animals is obscene' Julius said.

'But that's not what I meant. I saw the lobster on the top of the pile had one small still claw but its other was large as a paddle and kept lashing out at me in despair. I could almost hear its thirst for the sea. And yet I was fascinated by these dark cavernous heads and this great grey paddle swinging out on top; a great warty carbuncled cricket bat struggling to hit

19

the ball.'

There was a pause and then Julius said: 'Yes, I'm coming more and more to believe that we don't need to kill animals.'

'But that's not what I felt then' you said. 'I meant their travail was so slow and laboured and mute and blind. They reminded me of — I felt we are like them, clambering for ever slowly up piles of hard shells like crockery in search of the sea where we come from and never finding it. It is the story of my life since C.N.D.'

But Julius was saying: 'The future is with the vegetarians' and Thelma still sipping slowly at her first sherry added:

'I agree with Julius. Sooner or later men will find that they don't need to eat meat.'

Julius hummed and went into the garden and peed on some marigolds and pretended to wash his hands over the wallflowers. Annick was a clarinettist and you started to talk about a modern concerto she had been playing in under the conductor Annery. It was called 'Worlds' and the musicians were all dressed in black vests like Fascist bruisers and heavies, with Annery in the middle like Mosley on a swivelling rostrum swinging round to point at strings, wind, piano and clarinet in turn, and to get from each a few doodles with Annick moving about from 'World' to 'World' above the oboes' constant reedy toots. The young audience it had been written for shrieked their applause after each visit of the clarinet to the groups of instruments.

'Mind blowing' Julius who had been there came back in, 'if' giving you a deep bow 'if memsahib will permit us to appreciate anything more modern than Hindemith.'

'What do you think of this John Wersby quartet we are going to start rehearsing tomorrow?'

'I've privately christened him "Hop skip and jump out of the top floor window".'

'Which of his works were you thinking of?' you asked.

'Oh anything. All of them.'

'Not the song-cycle?'

'Not especially.'

'What then?'

'I can't put a name to all his works off hand. Was it the

20

Toccata or the Serenade?'

'One piece isn't as good as another' you cried angrily. 'Any more than one word is. Or one note is. You can't say "pheasant or wren" or "cock or eagle" any more than you can say one note is as good as another. You can't paraphrase a piece of music and in the same way you can't generalise about what people write or compose.'

'Sorry memsahib' Julius grimaced.

'It's all right Julius' Thelma said. 'Will is gradually becoming disenchanted with music. Beethoven bores him. Schoenberg he curses.'

You said nothing. You wanted her tight again.

Thelma produced a cheesecake she had bought on her way out to Thorley.

'Cheesecake! What is that?' Julius pretended not to know of such bourgeois foods. 'Do we spoon it or fork it?'

'What's the village like here?' Thelma asked.

'Oh I hate country life. The church and the manor house. Do people in other countries — in France for example, Annick — have to submit to Christian bell-ringing for two hours every Sunday evening? And the Vicar! I sit outside the church on Sunday evenings in my bare feet and call out "Hi!" as they come out of Evensong. Then the Vicar waves back: "Hi, Julius!" and the Lord and Lady of the manor salute me: "Good evening Mr Felix . . . Good evening Sir James. He'll only drink brandy out of Waterford glass. Ugh! I hate country life.'

'If you don't like the Vicar and the Lord of the manor' Annick protested, 'why do you sit there outside their church waiting for their greetings?'

'Village ways. Detestable as they are. Bourgeois. Inauthentic. In bad faith.'

'But it's insincere, it's you being inauthentic to say "Hullo" and stop to talk to people you don't like' Thelma added. Julius padded over the room eating a raw onion.

'Oh I believe in the civilities. One has to wear one's mask well. Otherwise society would collapse. But it is the obeisance of despair.'

He began to dust the windowsill and the table with his

21

sleeve. 'Pardon memsahib' he said to you. 'I don't get much time to clean very often and I don't believe in getting the lower orders to do my dirty work for me. You in your spotless Edwardian mansions must find it all a bit below par. And how is London? How is the great wen?'

'There are toads in the churchyard gardens' you said. 'Now toads again like lobsters and spider crabs . . .'

'Really?' Julius opened his eyes very wide. 'How mind blowing. But how are the people? Is it true that Alex has left the Party? And that Gillian Crowmarsh is getting a divorce? Someone told me she was living with Bruce Charpentier.'

'Things are moving then' said Thelma. 'And how was New Zealand and Australia?'

Julius shrugged. He had been touring there recently.

'What are the rocks like in New Zealand?' you asked, trying to join in.

'Big and black and strong and sometimes they open up and swallow people in. There was this C.P. member driving along and talking about the conquest of nature when she just disappeared. The road just opened up and took her in.'

'So much for the conquest of nature' said Thelma still sipping at her first sherry. She had not said 'If you get my meaning' or 'If you see my drift' once so far. She sat there poised and attractive and laughing as though to dissociate herself from you and your crabs and toads and fire-precautions. 'Jack Anderson is having an analysis.'

'I hate psycho-analysis. It erodes one's aspirations.'

'And the Forsters are having another baby.'

'How I hate babies.'

'So do I' said Thelma. 'Nasty jelly blobs.' You were eating a lunch of rice and bean shoots and stewed apples.

'I'm still hungry' said Thelma.

'Have some apricots.'

'Oh no. Too cold.'

'Let me open a tin of rice pudding.'

'Still too cold.'

'What about some cornflakes?'

'Yes cornflakes are warm.'

'I wonder why cornflakes are warm' you said.

'Yes, I wonder why.'

'Yes, I wonder why.' Julius rolled his eyes up in search of wisdom. Your words echoed round the room. Outside the new green leaf threatened to absorb you, standing stark against a grey steely sky. You could hear yourself talking about chalky soil retaining the heat. The Laurentian Shield. The isotherms round Lake Superior. You could hear yourself talking about house prices, fees for recitals and suddenly asking: 'Is rice an extra in Chinese restaurants?'

And at each struggling little remark it was as though a cold hard stone had been dropped into the conviviality. After each remark Julius would roll up his eyes and search for wisdom. You could hear yourself as though you were reading out of the Guinness Book of Records: '. . .an eighty-pound sturgeon . . . a starfish with ten limbs and a man weighing twenty-five stone.'

'Really' Julius would say. 'Is that so Herr Professor?'

A silence came down over the table. You could hear each other eating.

'Julius' Thelma suddenly interrupted it, 'how can we help Will get his love of music back? How can we winkle him out of his shell and get him back to where he was during the great days of C.N.D.?'

It was three o'clock. Julius stood at the larder squeezing up raisins in his fingers and squashing them into his mouth. Some fell on the floor. He trod on them with his bare feet and scraped up the flat sticky pad and put it into his mouth. He chopped up raw mushrooms and cucumber into a saucer and poured oil and vinegar over them and ate some with his fingers, feeding dense slices of mushroom like raw liver into Thelma and Annick's mouths. He accidentally spilled his purse full of money over them, and picked at them with a fork, separating out the pennies and the halfpennies and asking:

'Tell me Will. Tell me Thelma. Who orchestrates the newspapers? Who is the mind . . . which is the thermostat that tells "them" when to switch us off? Who advises the Home Secretary as to when we are and when we are not dangerous? Who advises the newspapers to treat C.N.D. as a joke and not a threat? Who *does* orchestrate the newspapers? I've written a pamphlet on the subject to be put out by the young at street corners.' Annick had gone into the kitchen to make some coffee. 'I want your advice' he lowered his voice. 'What would you think if a man of my age set up a scene with a girl twenty years younger?' He laughed shyly. 'Me with my eighteen-year-old daughter with all her father's hang-ups, setting out again with a girl of twenty-two?'

'Oh you mean Annick? But you don't mean marriage?' Thelma exclaimed.

'Yes' Julius laughed shyly. 'Don't tell George though. Nothing is settled. But do you think we could set up a scene together?'

'Wait till she hangs her pants to dry over your Gauguin, and her bra over your piano' Thelma said.

'I'd love that.'

'Or when she drops her eyebrow tweezers into the F-holes of your viola' Julius giggled as though he were being tickled.

'And your children throw bread and peanut butter at you when you are trying to practise.'

'Oh I could manage that.'

Once you had heard him say in a tête-à-tête with Thelma: 'Feeling a bit low? How about a bit of innocent, lighthearted, relaxed and loving promiscuity?' But this afternoon he was saying: 'Do you think with all my hang-ups and incestuous attitudes to my grown-up daughter, do you think Annick and I . . . ?' Annick came back.

'A friend of mine has just come back from Amsterdam with a polycarpus' she was saying. 'It's a fantastic thing. About this high.' She waved her hands above her head. 'And it keeps on growing. Soon it will touch the ceiling.'

'What's a polycarpus like?' you asked.

'I don't know' Annick dropped her hands and looked abashed. 'I've never seen one.' But you had cheated too. You already knew what a polycarpus looked like.

'Have you both got an hour or two free now?' Julius asked. 'I thought we might share a joint, and have a little re-education of the senses.' He got out a glass jar and put it on a tray on his knees. 'Who'd like to smoke? Though I myself don't

24

really need it.'

'I do' said Thelma.

'So do I.'

Julius was sitting on the sofa with a red cloth spread lovingly over his tray and he was carefully kneading the grass. Thelma had asked him several times to put her in touch with his pusher, his connection. But he would only shake his head:

'I couldn't really, could I? It wouldn't be fair on my daughter. I get it through her but not from her if you see what I mean.' He took a pin from his jeans and carefully picked together the threads and strands of the grass that had separated themselves from his cache.

'Don't you trust us then?'

'Of course I do. It's just that . . . and after all, a joint is a joint affair and I promise you we'll soon have another smoke.'

You all four sat in front of the television screen with the sound turned off. Just moving bodies on the screen and a tape-recorder playing Balinese music, drums and gongs and bells. Julius fed the green-brown seed of the grass into a cigarette paper, going lovingly round his tray with the pin, picking up stray bits. Then he tore the filter off a cigarette and fixed it at the end of the joint, lit up and slewed his mouth round to take in air with a hawking sound and held it there for about a minute and then exhaled and handed it to Thelma.

You sat in a row in front of the now mysterious television screen passing the joint from hand to hand, inhaling with great hawks and loud suckings of air, then passing it on and leaning back hand in hand to watch the bizarre rites taking place on the television.

At first you felt alarm. An arm swung out of the set at you with a bar of soap. Then the newscaster's eye looked at you personally and gave you a conspiratorial wink. Then women in flowered dresses with bare arms were standing about a room. The patterns on their dresses became jungles as you watched, serpents peered from under their armpits. Mangrove reached out of the set at you. And the women's dark eyes softened till they looked like lambs' kidneys and the black and white stripes of someone's tie became a grating through

25

which you could look into an unfathomable whiteness beyond. A grid between whose bars you could peer into a sea of light.

'Your dress is so beautiful' you said to Thelma knocking the rot off the joint and passing it on. The skin of your hand was a ploughed field speckled with seed. Each pore in Thelma's skin was a deep dark well waiting to have a great weight of moisture lowered down into its depths. Each root of your teeth was an aching tower. A tower of pleasure thrust up from the soft garden of the gums. The faces on the television screen stopped popping out at you and you saw the Prime Minister standing against a tower of crackly white salt which became an Aztec tomb then a Gothic cathedral with melting columns, a Gothic nave dripping and melting down into a pool that trickled away on to the floor, and fled into the cracks between the floor boards. Then a young man came forward with a cloth to mop the cathedral up, with a packet of J-cloths and an aerosol spray. He wrapped the cloth round him. He approached the cross where Jesus was being crucified. The soldiers standing round seized the piece of cloth he was wearing and stripped him of it so that he went away in nothing but a pair of underpants carrying a packet of Daz. The soldiers took squeegee mops and mopped up the blood under the cross. Then there was a massacre in a field full of hot poppies. Opium came running out of them and ran over the floor where the cathedral had melted and there was a smell of blood, sliced-up opium meat as they harvested, giving off blood.

You got up and left the room. You stood in the kitchen. Julius had put an old torn sheet on the kitchen chair. 'Oh look!' you said aloud. It had suddenly become a starched white choirboy surplice and you could see beautiful deep mauve shadows in its folds, like the shadows between the leaves of the trees outside. You looked at your jacket. The black buttons had become tunnels full of pitch reaching down to immense depths. You went to call the others. The door, as you turned the knob, gave out a beautiful tonic dominant sound. You wanted to stand there all day just turning the door-knob this way and that. You wandered into the bedroom. A very small spider lay on the windowsill watching a wasp caught in her Corbusier home built round the window-catch. Seeing that the wasp was far too big for her she pulled a trigger that released it. You could hear its sound. You killed the wasp and put it back in the web and the spider came back and dragged the corpse away and you could hear her loud crackling crunching as she chewed at her crustacean meat.

They had switched the television off when you got back to the living room. Julius and Annick and Thelma were still sitting hand in hand.

'Your hands feel like prickly pears, Julius' Thelma was laughing. The pot took her differently though. Julius was humming a hymn tune:

'That's the hymn I want at my funeral' she said, smiling dreamily. 'Only I shan't be there when you are all singing. I'll be being chopped up by handsome young medical students. Nice young medics at Bart's. The young men have already written and thanked me. A lovely letter. Told me I'd be a marvellous corpse. A marvellous bod' she went on dreamily. 'So while you're all singing, they'll be tossing an arm and a leg about. "Here. Catch! For you Tom." Tom is the name of the young medic who wrote and thanked me.' She spread herself over the sofa and fell into a dream.

There was silence after this speech. 'I'm thinking of erecting a windmill in my garden' Julius changed the subject. 'And a solar heater so that I can be entirely independent of the black fossil.'

'Black fossil?' Thelma was aroused. 'What's that?'

'Coal and electricity and gas. The whole basis of capitalist society.'

You wandered away into the garden. You could hear them talking:

'. . . Too fat to get out of the window on to the balcony to make his speech, so they had to say he'd been taken ill . . . They only got married for semantic reasons . . . Had a word with him when he asked for money: "Is this really how you want your life to be? If it is, here's the money for the booze" . . .' The voices faded.

You looked at some foxgloves and seemed able to enter

27

their mauve spotted caverns with black sexual tongues hanging out over you and lilting gently to the sound of bees. You wandered over to some sunflowers and gazed at their polished black seeds. The smell of lime leaves took you back to your mother's garden in Sussex when you were a child and she carried you out one night when you couldn't sleep. You wandered out of the garden and down the heavily scented lane. You came to a dark green pond. You sat down beside it, and it began to wink at you conspiratorially as the newscaster had done. And the May green foliage seemed to be creeping nearer and nearer to you, whispering that it was coming to take you, and you must surrender to it. You saw the crabs again on the hot dry stall in Chapel Market struggling mutely to reach the sea. You could hear their grinding claws as they rose and fell and heaved and dropped, and you left the green pool and went back to Julius's cottage.

The three of them were sitting in an apple tree when you got back. Julius was fumbling in a plastic bag and pulling out mungo beans and feeding them into Thelma and Annick's mouths, and chucking some down among the fallen blossom beneath them. They were talking about the Provisional Revolutionary Government of South Vietnam. Julius chucked mungo beans at you and cried:

'Great about the N.L.F. victory.'

'Yes' you replied. 'One always does want to see David overcome Goliath.'

'And Socialism overcome Capitalism.'

You nodded. 'Capitalism has taken a nasty blow.' He showered beans at you and you tried to play up and catch them or ward them off, but the gaze of the deep green pool came back, and the heavy, somnolent but suffocating green trees. You didn't want to try to play the game any more.

'I think we ought to be going' you called up to them.

' 'Tis but the third hour' Thelma called back. 'Still Will always likes to go to bed early, so perhaps we . . .'

'What a waste of the best hours of the day' Julius cried down. 'No one needs more than four hours' sleep. I sometimes take it lying on the sofa, sometimes lying in the garden among the flowers.'

28

'But Will gets in a panic' Thelma laughed, 'if he doesn't get his eight hours.'

'Four for a man. Five for a woman. And six for a fool' Julius finished off the beans. Thelma kissed him and climbed down the tree.

'A marvellous day. Thank you so much. Can you drop in after your rehearsal tomorrow?' Julius nodded:

'Bless you. I wish I were a woman.'

'Yes, I'm glad I'm a woman' Annick murmured drowsily.

'So am I' said Thelma. 'Perhaps Will should have been a woman too. He could have his eight hours' sleep then quite legitimately.'

'See you tomorrow.'

You drove along in silence.

'Today could have been a happy day' Thelma said at last.

'Wasn't it happy?' you asked bitterly.

'Julius talked about his work and his recital tours while you were out in the lanes. I wish your work would seize hold of you for a change.'

'Why do you say "could have been such a happy day"? You seemed unkindly happy at my expense.'

'If you hadn't always ruined everything by putting the brake on with some remark about fire precautions or electricity prices in Southern Ireland just as we were getting up a good discussion. Fire precautions indeed! And the rocks of New Zealand!'

'What did D.H. Lawrence say? . . . "A woman is like a violinist. Any fiddle. Any instrument rather than empty hands and no tune going".'

'You drag me down.'

'Ganging up with Julius and youth won't help to lift you up again.'

'You don't give me any licence to exist. Julius is the only one who does that.'

'Julius. He only wants an audience. Any ear will do. Julius was laughing at us the whole time.'

'Speak for yourself. Julius made me feel real. Crabs and toads and fire precautions!'

'I left the conversational ball to you. After all, I see Julius

29

almost every day. His chatter is just inspired glop. Would you like me to buy you a colour T.V. set? You seem rather restless and unhappy as soon as we are alone.'

'Yes. Or I could take up crochet and make mats to go on our tables, and covers to go round bottles of wine. And a shoulder cape for your cello. And I could go to the bingo up at King's Cross every Wednesday afternoon.'

'Now. Now. You know what I mean. You don't like shopping much. And you tend to get bored in the flat all day alone. And you seem slightly depressed every time we leave Julius or he leaves us.'

'But why can't you just . . .'

'I am not a public man. I don't ever feel very much togetherness. And I just can't and don't want to play the games that you play so beautifully with Julius and his friends. And you weren't even drunk. You and I, we . . . we . . . aren't like that.'

'I refuse to be clumped together with you in this "we". I enjoyed myself. I felt one of them. Annick was a nice young person. It was you who kept talking about isotherms and the Laurentian Shield. And the herrings all leaving the English Channel. I sometimes wonder what is going on in that shell of yours. Or if there is anything going on in there at all. Why don't you try to acquire some presence? Some personality? I could hear you droning on all the time. That makes me unhappy.'

'Who cares about happiness? Are those geraniums on the windowsill of that cottage over there happy? Is the tap happy because you turn it on and release so much water? Who cares about happiness?'

'I do. Very much. But Will, who are our friends then if Julius and Annick aren't?'

'They have their lives and we have ours. But perhaps the reason why we haven't many friends is because I treat other people with less love than I ought. That is why I make such fatuous remarks at parties. I'm trying and I get punished for it.'

'But your music.'

'I am what I am, and my music is my business not yours.'

'But I want to share it with you but I can't.'

'I have just temporarily lost, temporarily I hope, lost the obsession that kept me going for nearly thirty years.'

'Is it because of the failure of C.N.D.? And Vietnam?'

'Partly, but Vietnam only triggered it off.'

'We were happy during C.N.D. But now you depress me with your cynicism and your contempt for other people. You have even turned away from other musicians.' She had not said 'If you see my meaning . . . If you get my drift' once today. 'And you have turned away from ordinary people.'

'I don't count hob-nobbing with pressers and oversewers and people whose way of life is profoundly different from ours as anything more than ugly patronage. Nothing but an affront to them. The people living in Holborn and Clerkenwell don't want Mr and Mrs Parrish's patronage.'

'Who are our friends then, if Julius isn't?' she asked wide-eyed as though it had just dawned on her. 'Tell me who they are.'

'I don't count shouting across noisy cocktail parties as being with friends. You have no sense of the "Other" in other people. I am I and I'm not like you and Julius and I don't regard dropping in unannounced into other people's flats or screaming remarks over drinks about speed limits and parking-problems and holidays in Spain as friendship any more than you used to. But things won't get any easier as the years go on and society becomes more informal. It will become more difficult to cultivate the old-fashioned virtues of hospitality when the formal rules have finally broken down.'

'So people avoid us. Afraid of being bored. Oh it's too lonely living with you. Now. You drag me down. Well, since we can't have mutual friends I must try to make friends of my own.'

'Yes, you do that, you must try to. But I can't improvise. I can't pretend. I can't lose my sense of what my "isness" is, where meeting people is concerned. But you. You always expect too much of other people. And they withdraw in fear. Or you withdraw in disgust because they won't study Plato's Forms or take up the flute.'

31

'You have always hated my flute.'

'I've grown tired of that Mozart slow movement played like "The Last Rose of Summer".'

'And I'm tired of telling you that it is not the Mozart slow movement but a composition of my own.'

'Passion without technique sounds particularly mawkish on a flute.'

'I hope you don't treat your pupils as you treat me,' Thelma said at last, 'killing them every time they offend your aesthetic sense.'

'It's the bad habits I try to kill. Not the person.'

'I hope they appreciate the difference.'

'Young men very quickly learn to detach their egos, themselves, their vanities from their musical ideas.'

'Only the ones who come from musical families do.'

'No. The young man from the Northern Grammar School learns as well. It's the first thing you learn at a conservatoire.'

'I hope your girl students learn how to despatch their egos as well. George never treats his pupils with such contempt. Perhaps that's why you don't have all that many pupils.' You winced.

'I deliberately keep my teaching hours down. You know I do. To practise and to be with you.'

You drove on in silence. 'That settles it' you said at last. 'I shall turn down that invitation to the States. Not because of your drinking. It's simply a matter of several thousand dollars less than they paid Julius on his last tour.'

'Why worry about a few thousand dollars? We are well off. And the children have their scholarships. We don't need all that money. So why worry about a few thousand dollars?'

You stopped the car. 'Do you think that at my age I'm going to be treated as Julius's inferior?'

'Well, you're not half so well known as he is, and you've played less in public.'

'You mean I am less distinguished than he is?'

'Yes' she said humbly. 'Your name isn't so well known.'

'Ever since I joined the quartet you have treated me as George and Nancy and Julius's inferior.' She was silent. 'Why do women always have to judge men by how they shape up

32

against other men?' She was still silent then she burst out:

'Why do men have to be so self-important as to worry about their male prestige — their masculine pride — because they are offered a few thousand dollars less than another man would be? Your self-respect is based so shallowly. I'm glad I'm a woman. Men's competitiveness! Great artists don't bother about how they measure up against other men. They measure themselves against the music alone.'

'You still haven't answered my question. You do think I'm inferior as a musician and a person to Julius.'

'I am no judge about music.'

'You treat me as less distinguished.'

'I sometimes can't help adopting your own self-valuation and seeing you as you see yourself.'

'And how do I see myself?' She didn't want to reply. 'Answer my question.'

'Why do you want an answer to it?'

'Because today I've seen you as you really are when you're not under the influence. You don't love me or respect me.' She said nothing. 'For the last five years you've treated me like this. And when I see you with other people I see you as you really are. A shallow, flirtatious, falsely animated manic ganger up. You like to hunt with the hounds even if the quarry is your husband. You treat me as second rate as soon as we are with other people. Today I've seen you as you really are.'

'And today I've seen you as you really are. Boring and unimportant. That's why I drink. Not because I have no friends. Not because I've got no work. But because you're asleep.'

'Cruel, arrogant and self-important' you thought aloud. 'Dull and boring. Asleep.'

'We'll try to get you moving again.' Thelma touched you softly. You winced. 'We'll try to get you put back on the map.'

'Try not to invade me like that. Leave me some inner space to call my own.'

'It is you who invade me. You never allow me an inch to be other than a mother and a housewife. My talk is all chatter. If I am silent it is suppressed anger. If I am animated it is flirtatious glop.'

'Nothing has any value except that which is not us. I offer you that free space and you drink instead of exploring it.'

'I drink partly to fantasise myself out of the boredom of an unlived life, and partly . . .'

'And partly?'

'Julius calls your playing low-pitched tittering in a corner.'

'How thoughtful of you to repeat it to me.'

'You asked me why I drink. I drink because of my anxiety and depression about you. As I said before I can't help taking over your own self-valuation and making it mine.'

'And what is that self-valuation?'

'You know that you have lost your artistic skills. You know you have lost your love of music.' You winced at the simplicity of the verdict. 'How can I love my husband if I can't respect him? Nothing works for you any more. That is why I drink. I feel so guilty at you playing in such a famous quartet as the Tavistock and . . .'

'And not being up to it? Is that what you mean?'

'That is why I drink.' Then she added: 'Oh Will, I'm so afraid. They want to see you out of the quartet. Why not get a job in a really good orchestra. Even you could be leader of a London symphony orchestra.'

'Even you.' The green round you suddenly moved forwards towards you.

' "Even you". Do you despise me so much?'

'If you got a job in an orchestra . . .'

'And in any case it isn't my love of music as you so judiciously put it that I have lost. It's my obsession with non-tangible good. I have just temporarily lost my obsession with disrelation. I temporarily despair of being able to bridge the gulf between the outer world of speech and action and things. Wars. And the inner world of triumph over them. Every artist goes through patches of dryness.'

'Yes, it's like monks and nuns and mystics' she put her arm round you. 'I hope we'll pull you through it soon.'

'I feel like a parched rubber tyre. My mouth is full of hard dry bread crumbs that stick in my throat, dry and prickly. And unnourishing. I feel like the deposit in a kettle. Help me!

34

Help me!' You sat quite still in the car. The evening green gazed in at you with a wicked eye, hooded by a thunderous black sky. It seemed to stand all round the car, just waiting. 'Help me!'

'I'm sorry' Thelma was saying. 'I didn't mean to erode your morale like that. I know things are bad and I'm going to try and help to get them better. I must show you more love. Instead of getting tight and you pitying me, you becoming my nurse, I'm going to forget my own trivial worries and help you get your musical obsession back. First I think it may be because since Vietnam you have cut yourself off from other people. I'll stop drinking. I'll go on the wagon. We'll have people in like we used to.'

You drove on. You tried to change the subject. You mentioned a Dvořák concert that you had given.

'It was two years ago, not this last summer' Thelma was saying. 'Your memory! Your forgettery. And you used to know it by heart, and now you have to take the music in with you. I'll have to have a blitz on you. We'll get you round. Things will get stuck together again. Things will start to grow once more in your brain. I'm going to try and winkle you out of your shell. I'm going to help you quench your thirst by not drinking. I'm going to get you out of that shell of yours' she repeated as your mother used to say.

' "People who make calls on other people's souls are bound to find the door shut". You have no feeling for my "isness". You simply want me to be like other men and I am not. You take over their valuation of me. You leave me no room to move.'

But Thelma was implacable in her revenge: 'I'm not going to drink any more. I need to be clear-headed and sober to get you out of this slough of despond.'

You were passing a signpost to the villages of Happenden and Offenden near where you had once lived as a child.

'Let's make a detour' Thelma said as you stopped at the cross-roads, hungrily. 'Happenden, Offenden, Bligh Woods and Pound Common . . .' images that came back to you and could neither be expanded or contracted. Images that were neither to be interpreted or suppressed. You saw the signpost

35

nostalgically. There no one could invade your inner space as Thelma did sober. You would go there as soon as the Cambridge recital was over, and without telling a soul. You would turn the bend and find the water.

'We could have a picnic there one day' Thelma was saying. 'Fields and trees and countryside. Perhaps that is what you need. We will go. I promise you. We will go.'

You dreamed that night that piles of rags were lying under your windows and an old woman was shouting up at you that they were yours and that you must take them up to the hospital. But the room in the hospital where you were told to take them was full of doctors and nurses all walking along the ceilings and the walls and they sent you downstairs to a likelier place, a basement canteen with splashed tables and plastic lily-cups with cigarettes stubbed out in them. And you were at the counter asking for three lambs' hearts but they corrected you: 'Three lambs' chests' and handed you a bundle wrapped in newspaper and when you opened it there was an Indian's hand inside, wrenched off at the wrist and smelling of menstrual blood.

You sat up in bed. It was four in the morning. Thelma went on sleeping. You lay down again and she was pumping your cello up until it became a great pair of hips caging a huge uterus waiting for impregnation. The F-holes suddenly held ovaries bursting out seed. You and Thelma had not made love for two years now. She pretended she didn't mind. Perhaps she didn't, you reflected. Now. After the day at Thorley, and the conversation you had coming home.

She lolled over in her sleep and shifted away from you. It was five. A pang like an explosion woke you every morning now at five. You were forty-five. You were fifty. You were sixty. Every morning when you woke you had passed another year of your life.

You got up and went into the kitchen and made some coffee. You didn't want to go back to the bedroom in case your dream came back when you lay down on the pillow and it took your head and shaped it back into the mould of last night.

You would wake up sometimes in dread that you would

36

miss your train or that Thelma would let squatters in while you were away on tour. Or you would miss an entry. Or the concert hall was empty. Or you had broken a string and had to play on three. 'The quartet wants to ease you out' Thelma had said. 'But I am going to put you back in the swim once more.' You stood at the window looking out into the church-yard, looking at the trees that were waiting for you out there. I can no longer play well. One day I will just stop being able to play at all.

CHAPTER III

George, the first violin, would be the first to arrive at the Gordon Hall where you rehearsed. 'Hi!' he would sit there repeating a long cantabile passage again and again, nodding over his violin as you came in: 'Hi!' He was the oldest of the quartet, tall and thin with a shock of white hair and strong white hairs stalking from his nostrils which he fingered when he thought. 'Hi!' he nodded over his violin when you came in: 'Just starting to undo this lovely cantabile. How art thou?'

Then Julius arrived with his viola: 'Sorry I'm late but the dog got run over in the night. It was a lovely way to go though. He had been out all night pleasuring the girls. I hope I die that way too . . .' Julius pushing back his long lanky black hair that hung down to his chest and putting his viola under his chin. He had his wild pagan delinquent look on as he pushed his tongue out and nibbled at the corners of his mouth and frowned and played an arpeggio like a puzzled Amerindian new to the idea of diatonic music: 'I've just killed three people with one bomb and had four cups of tea.' George nodded. You stood against the wall smoking and standing your cigarette upright on the windowsill while you tuned up.

Then Nancy, the second violin, arrived. She was always late. She would arrive breathlessly with her dog and two large supermarket carriers bulging with packets of cornflakes and meat loaf. She would hook the dog's lead under her chair:

'Basket, sit down! Good Basket.' The dog was sick and she had to take him to the vet at four this afternoon. She fumbled in her carriers for a dog biscuit: 'So I shall have to love

38

you and leave you at four.'

'That doesn't give us much time for the John Wersby then. Can't someone else take Basket to the vet?'

'The kids don't get out of school till four, and Jack is away in Glasgow till next week.'

'Art thou ready?' George looked round at you as Nancy got her breath and tuned up. She was careless about tuning, careless about practising. She had a street face, roughly put together, amorphous, thin, snub-nosed, with dark shadows under her eyes like a newspaper vendor pale with standing at the street corner all evening in the exhaust fumes of the cross-roads crying: 'Late Night Finals'. Her playing was abrupt, jerky and awkward. Her arms were plump and short and she would struggle with getting the right arm across the bridge of her violin with a rugged battling defiance. But she had a beautiful tone and would lead up to climaxes of sudden boldness and conviction where her accidental face became suddenly moulded with disciplined passion.

'Art thou ready?' George repeated. 'We don't want to lose the tempo of this movement as we did last week. What think you, Julius?'

> 'Hurrah! Hurrah! The first of May.
> Outdoor sex begins today'

Julius sang running his bow up and down his rosin. 'Yes, let's not lose the tempo.' He hummed and beat time with his foot.

George nodded. There was strength in his playing but always behind it something cosy and homecoming; something reassuring which made him hostile to atonalism. 'Surely' he would say, 'this passage is saying "How are you? Well or ill? Let me sing to you".' Or: 'And this passage is the voice of widows and orphans.'

'In Vietnam?' Nancy would ask. She had tried several times to get the quartet to give a recital to raise funds for 'Medical Aid To Vietnam'. But George always stood out against the idea:

'We are not here to take sides.'

'I suppose you never took sides in the Second World War?

Or during the bombing of London?'

'Well, it would be a poor lookout for us artists here if we had a Communist government to play under.'

'It's up to us to create Socialism with a human face.'

'As they tried to in Czechoslovakia. Still let's not tangle now. And this passage is about friendship and humanity' he would continue, putting himself between the music and the listener and imposing his own homely humanism on them.

'George's music is larded with fat' Julius would complain.

You began with the second movement of the Haydn. Julius stopped you. 'A little less bravissimo, Will. Don't you think? I've got a feeling that the cello is only accompanying till we get to the second crescendo.'

'What think you, Will?' George asked.

'Perhaps.' You spoke for the first time that morning. You began the passage again. A thin spiteful hissing sound came from the belly of your cello and poured into your left ear:

'We'll get you back. We'll get rid of that dryness. We'll have people in. I'll stop boozing and we'll soon have you out of that shell. Only you must try, Will. You must try to come alive again. We'll give you a helping hand up. But we can't do it alone.' You were playing a delicate line of inquiry with the first violin: 'Is it so?' . . . 'Just so.' A neat careful clean dialogue, but your mind wandered to the window. Green pressed its flat hands lovingly against the panes. Flat hands, open hands, waiting for you . . . Did she despise you so much when she was sober?

'Oh Will!' George cried. 'Where wert thou? You muffed that delicious little conversation. And Nancy, you had better leave that piece of joinery and sort it out later on your own.'

'Yes. The shitwork of this movement can be done alone,' Nancy agreed.

'Let's go from bar sixty-four' Julius pulled back his hair. His playing was so transparent, so full of what he was interpreting that you would forget the Julius of Thorley as he played. He became nothing but a door opening on to a great encounter. He was the mastermind of the quartet.

You rehearsed the Haydn for about an hour then Nancy put down her bow:

'This Haydn' wrinkling up her nose, as though she were smelling a persistent bad smell. 'I find this movement so gratuitous.' She fingered her mousy brown hair and re-wrapped her long Indian skirt. 'So unearned. Always sailing with the wind behind it. Taking the line of least resistance. This is Haydn at his worst and he said so himself.'

'I read the opposite, that he liked it,' George replied. 'I gathered that Haydn was very pleased with it.'

'He probably was financially' Nancy grimaced. 'But it's pianistic stuff really.'

'And a lousy transcription' Julius added. 'Listen to this run. Tra-la-la.'

'It doesn't give us anything. He did it for money. Plonkety-plonk.'

'Maybe you're thinking too musically. Not technically enough,' George peered over his score. 'To me the movement says "Where are you?" . . . "I am here." . . . like a child first learning to walk.'

> 'Baby's first Christmas,
> He's covered in blood' (Julius sang)
> 'Mother don't want him.
> Father's inside.'

'Still a bit unsteady. Like a dog looking for his master' George ignoring him went on.

'Oh really George!' Nancy put down her bow.

'She was the Queen of the Mardi Gras' Julius sang. 'That's what it says to me. Shall we break for coffee after the Allegretto?'

'But there's still a nasty squalid sound somewhere' Nancy frowned. 'A really grotty shitty sound.' They looked at you. Your brain felt like two codeine tablets being rubbed together. There was ground glass on your fingertips when you played; grit and cigarette ash on your bow, and your rosin felt made of clinker.

'A nasty shitty sound' Nancy frowned.

'Wait till we start rehearsing the John Wersby then,' George muttered. 'It's like a dog lifting his leg and peeing on us each in turn.'

41

'Wasn't he the composer in residence at Cambridge before he died?'

'That's why we are doing it there.' You made coffee and sipped it.

'Art thou ready?' George called wiping coffee from round his mouth. 'Opus 130. Bar thirty-three. And let's not be in danger of turning that carefree bit of staccato into a careless bit of mish-mash.'

'Yes, and let's try and get that lovely line at bar forty-seven a bit cleaner. Let's get it like a ripe peach falling off its stone.'

'And we haven't quite unpicked those triplets yet. Let's get them moving freely. Liberate them. And there's no connection yet with Will's bottom D.'

'And we've let the first movement get a rather dragging beat and if we simply repeat it here we're in danger of simply referring backwards instead of leading into the *alla tedesca*.'

'What are we going to play in Sydney?' Nancy was asking. 'Have we decided yet?'

'If we ever get to Sydney' Julius drummed on the belly of his viola.

'Why shouldn't we get there?'

But none of them dared to say that you were playing your cello like a sewing machine with a handle to turn at the side and producing an even flow of monotonous taut threads. Or that Nancy would go away and fail to do the 'shitwork' of the work. Or that George would play the Cavatina of the Beethoven Opus 130 too fulsomely, trying to compensate for the rest of you and to paper over the rift that was beginning to open between the members of the quartet.

'Let's look at the Cavatina' George suggested when you had washed up your coffee things and returned to the hall. You opened with George's long melody; there were tears in his eyes. ' "Never have I written a melody that affected me so much" ' he quoted Beethoven. 'He composed it with sorrow and tears and even the memory of it brought tears to his eyes.'

You played the beautiful moving movement. It brought a high white crying to your ears, as though each time the water

42

came to lift you, it only lapped at you and then receded, and you were left with an ocean in your ears which you could never reach. Miles of dry shingle lay between you and the place where you wanted to be. The waters were coming. You could hear their whispering rustle, but they always came only so far and you were left on the parched dry white wind-swept shingle.

'Why not let's play it on four piano accordions?' Julius stopped you angrily. 'We could at least turn it into something, even if it's only a Music Hall turn.'

'We're not in the right mood for it obviously today' George agreed sadly. 'Let's put it aside for the moment and look at the John Wersby.'

You all looked moodily and gloomily at the photostated copies that Julius pushed round. 'If only we could read the wretched thing. If only, for instance, I knew whether that first note was supposed to be a G sharp or a G natural at bar nine.'

'Let's go straight through it' Nancy suggested, ' and get a rough idea of it, and then we can start to unpick it after lunch.'

'Right.' George put his glasses on, pulled them down his nose and looked at his copy. You struggled through the first movement. It was full of pauses. 'Like Gruyère cheese, all full of holes' Julius nibbled at his mouth, as he always did when he was faced with a problem. You played the second move-ment. It was a bizarre grotesque dance. The last movement was wild and agitated, then suddenly it broke into a strange tonal tune. George put down his bow:

'Phew! Is this all his agent could produce?'

'Have the same girl twice and you are in danger of becom-ing a member of the establishment' Julius grinned. 'That's what it says to me. And we'll have the bogs painted blue for the masses . . . And who has been shitting in the Queen's shoes?'

'We can't play this' George shook his head. 'I'm sure Wersby was very sincere. But conviction by itself doesn't make art. It has its moments, but on the whole it would be unfair to him.'

'I disagree' said Nancy. 'You want him to write like Elgar or Vaughan Williams and he isn't. This is an innocent seeing eye, and the sudden capsules of silence make you hear sounds as if for the first time.'

You went on rehearsing the strange, strident, discordant sounds till you came to the strange disconcerting tonal, almost ecclesiastical tune at the end.

'By God, that's sad' George admitted. 'It's a bit like the end of Berg's "Lyric Suite".'

'Let's eat.' You all four crossed Theobald's Road and went into an Italian restaurant.

'Well, yes, I suppose I agree with you in principle' George said apropos nothing, waving his glasses over the spaghetti he was eating till they steamed over. He wiped them carefully. 'But I don't think we are ready for anarchism yet, Nancy. We haven't got that far yet. For instance, there was this place down at Cookham Dean where we spent our holidays during the war. They were all anarchists and they never stopped quarrelling once. Their children's hair was always so dirty that we could never let our kids play with them, and their clothes were handwoven out of bits of wool they picked off the hedges. And the poor kids always looked so cold that one day we threw them out a blanket. And some meat. I know it was very wrong of us since they were vegetarians and only ate berries. But they looked so under-nourished and cold in the things they wove – well, I don't know what you would call them – saris I suppose.'

'Ha! I see.' Nancy put down her fork. 'Of course, that was why Franco won the Civil War in Spain. He was just fighting nice pacifist free-thinking middle-class men and women gathering berries in homespun saris. Why talk about anarcho-syndicalism, George, when you're so ignorant about it?'

'Sorry,' he smiled and swung his glasses from the tape that held them round his neck. 'No. I just don't know what the answer is to power. Except music. Perhaps that is what the Wersby is trying to say' he pretended to muse. 'Sorry. I'm just one of the millions of "don't knows". Not my field. Sorry.'

Nancy was clenching and unclenching her feet in her

44

slippers under the table. She bit her lip.

'But I doubt if this music of Wersby's will convert them all to pacifism' George mused on.

'No one's mentioned pacifism' Nancy ground her teeth.

'Really? Oh I'm sorry. I thought that was what the Campaign for Nuclear Disarmament was all about.'

'I'm not a pacifist and I never have been.' George twirled his glasses and let them fall into his pasta.

'I ought to know better. Sorry.'

'You know as well as I what Unilateralists believe.'

'Well' George gazed at the ceiling, 'perhaps we're all anarchists at heart.'

'So we are! Even the Queen is. Even our Prime Minister is at heart.'

George put his glasses on. 'Well, as you know, I'm not an expert in these things. But it does seem to me and I hate to say it after all the marching and leafletting that you and Will and Thelma have done in late years . . . I hate to say it but it does seem to me that we have survived so far because of this wretched Bomb.'

'Why do you call it wretched then? You should be hymning its praises on May morning out at Rickmansworth. It's your best friend.'

'No. No. But seriously, why do you get so bugged up by it all? What about the fair laws we have got? What about our free schools and free hospitals? And our free press? Who's responsible for them if not your so-called "Capitalist Oppressors"?'

'Oh George, you know that Hitler was far better than us at all that. The state will do you proud for as long as you can work . . . For as long as you're prepared to disguise yourself as some part of the vegetable kingdom.'

George put his head on one side: 'So you think there is a revolution brewing? I wonder.'

'There might have been in 1961 if the Labour Party had stayed with us.'

'But we seem to have survived so far.'

'What makes you think we have? I don't feel I have. The only ones who have survived are the ones who don't care

45

tuppence about dignity and freedom and life. The ones who are content to be kept by Auntie B.B.C. in fleecy-lined cages marked "Handle with Care . . . Keep free from Despondency and Alarm." The only people who have survived are the ones who have frozen themselves into their environment and have sealed themselves off against the possibility of change.'

'Yes, well. All right then. But why not resign yourself to the higher interests of the state? At least we have a free press here and no Siberia.'

'Mid-air civilisation doesn't need camps and Siberia. Ours oppress their citizens by deliberately lowering their consciousness. Except for the élite, we're like a lot of people in a massive Twilight Home for the Aged. We just sit there in our wheel-chairs half-grumbling, half-terrorized by the staff, but somehow compliant and acquiescing while Auntie B.B.C. rumbles out the news:

' "Bank Holiday and trippers set out in even larger numbers again this year, but our correspondents thought they detected signs of strain and anxiety on some of the holiday-makers' faces as they made their way to their favourite beaches; partly perhaps because of the warm spell coming so soon after a long hard winter and spring; and partly perhaps because of the recent price increases. But as their day got under way, the holiday-makers caught on to the holiday spirit and their anxiety began to give way to a keen sense of enjoyment. They began to eat hot dogs and queue for the iced lollies and deck-chairs that had been set out for them along the beaches. And in the Royal Parks. By the end of the day thousands of deck-chair tickets had been sold and tons of sunburn lotion and iced-lollies." '

'Christmas' said Julius, 'And the Postmaster General has announced that the four thousand children who had sent letters to Santa Claus through the postal services again this year would not be disappointed . . . Hiroshima Day and it's a tight spot for girls. On their way to work this morning they all lost their tights when a chemical was released from a nearby lens factory. "They literally ran down our legs" the girls said. "We felt awful when we felt our tights trickling away" they giggled on the television screen. However, an apology

46

has come from the factory and each girl is to receive a new pair of tights and a frozen chicken to take home as well. And that is all from the newsroom. Goodnight.'

'Time we were going back' said George.

'That's how I interpret the John Wersby' said Nancy getting up.

'But then why did he just go off and do himself in?' You looked from face to face; from Nancy to George to Julius. How much longer would they tolerate you in the quartet? Your mouth had felt dry as they talked. It was full of dust and ashes. Oily screws and rusty pins stood before your eyes, and blotched plastic bags. And the feel of typewriter ribbons and carbon paper was on your fingers. You were crossing the Theobald's Road. You were afraid that George might suggest going back to the Beethoven − the theme they took up so eloquently and you played with your tongue in your cheek. A thin membrane would hang between you and the Opus 130. So thin you thought you could, but never did, succeed in piercing it. You waited as the insomniac waits for sleep. You waited as the beached crab waits for high tide to sweep over it and engulf it. But the tide only lifted you so far and dropped you back where you had been. You played struggling to be lifted and carried, lifted and swept away, but only the feeling of parchedness came, communicating itself from your brain to your shoulder and from your shoulder to your arm and your hand and your bow. It was when you tried to get over this dryness that you played exaggeratedly, as though your tongue were in your cheek.

'Too much bravissimo' Julius would complain, and then you would lapse into your sewing-machine stitches . . . ('Oh give my roots rain').

You started rehearsing the John Wersby again.

'That E sharp of yours sounds like a nasty little cheap Jap coffee grinder just setting off on its morning task.'

'This is a lovely phrase. Let's tell it as though it were the beginning of a story' George sighed. 'Once upon a time . . . but she died . . .'

'If you want to give it that kind of buttery grace . . .'

'But it's coming on.'

'Yes but we're giving it about as much body as a fried jelly-fish . . .'

You packed up at four and went home. But Thelma would be in so you turned into the little churchyard gardens beside the Royal Free Hospital and sat down by the Gothic mortuary covered in green bunting. The birds were bathing in the blossom above you. Blossom trickled and fell on you from the green meshing above. The old grey walls round the garden were swollen with green like green overfed cats creeping bulkily along their tops. Green meat was growing off the rickety crutched chimneys of the street in front of you. Green about to topple the grey fumey streets. Green waiting to take them down . . . For a moment you felt at peace and the green was nothing but a pleasant May pressure, a great surprise, an iconoclast climbing over 'Vernon Dictabelt Records' and 'Wyebone Soil Distributor'.

But as you sat there at peace thinking 'My music will come back with the same sudden green surprise' you began to think through the Wersby manuscript till you came to the haunting, faraway May morning tune that even George had been moved by this afternoon . . . its beginning as a simple, serene liturgical chant on the muted violins, then the cello entering to take the theme away, invert it, deprive it of all meaning by its broad deep staccato drumming: 'Thorns for thy head's remembrance.'

And you are standing by the river with your father when the big children have gone to school.

'Where does that path go to?' you are asking.

      ' "Into my heart an air that kills
      From yon far country blows" '

he replies standing by his shoes by the river.

'Is it very deep?' you ask. And he nods.

'Very.'

'If two of me were standing there one on the other's shoulders, would I reach the top and be able to breathe?'

And he says doubtfully: 'I doubt it.'

And you persist: 'Yes, but if there was you and mother standing with me on top would my head come up and be able to breathe?'

And your father shakes his head as if he doubts the survival of your parents and even yourself. You shake his hand but he only shakes his head.

'I doubt it.' And he is standing there beside his shoes weeping and then he is dead and calling to you from further down the river to come to him.

'I have found it. It is here.' And the shadow of a necessary death hangs over you, and you hear the Wersby May morning tune again.

A rickety metal trolley with parched rubber wheels is circling the churchyard gardens. Starlings are lifting bits of chopped sausage and cheese from the path. A breeze comes. The leaves are being stroked taut. Tugged. Reined in then caught in a sudden stillness which turns the traffic of the Gray's Inn Road to a distant plane droning in the sky. It is twilight. The chestnut lobes loom from their darkening corners. Their flowers are strained upwards. Their leaves are dragged down. You are caught by them, strained upwards and dragged down in the tension of their bursting red and green breasts. By the river you are standing. Or in the village school chanting:

'And He leads His children on
To the place where He is gone.'

A sudden message. A sudden gaze. A sudden opening. You think of the May morning tune again. It is in the key of A and it slides out suddenly, ecclesiastically, from the atonality of the work, like a hymn suddenly caught on a breeze from a nearby church, an organ playing, voices chanting, then it takes its terrible turn 'Thorns for thy head's remembrance' and what comes at the end is not the flooding in of joy or of renewal and recuperation but of terror and exile, touching something that lies beyond subjectivity, touching something much more ancient than God or the church or the self:

'Are these flowers or thorns that spring in all her majesty puts out? Flowers or the blind thorns' staring adornment? Dawn comes on this ancient world to take you.' And then like the shadow of a bomber over the tide of all this green, your father comes back and the shadow of a necessary death:

49

'Then die, Prince. Die!' The green is winking at you now conspiratorially. The green gaze comes again. The water is deep and grey-green and moving only enough to take you peacefully after your father and out of exile. The shadow of a necessary death has been with you ever since you were that child standing there by the river with your father weeping on the path to Happenden, Offenden, Bligh Woods and Pound Common.

CHAPTER IV

'Hew the Bad Tree down!' you would sing in your country school standing beside your desks on Monday mornings when the Vicar came in to take prayers and question each child who had been absent from church the day before. He always left the 'beach children' till the end. They lived on the beach road two miles from the village, in caravans and corrugated iron shacks and old railway carriages blistered by the sun and propped up on bricks and empty oil drums. Most of them went to the 'Radiance Mission Hall' on the beach road on Sundays.

'Please Sir,' they would stand up and touch their forelocks when the Vicar asked them where they had been yesterday, 'Radiance Hall.' The 'Radiance Hall' smelt of creosote and the sweet chemical reek of the rows of elsans in the communal W.C.s next door. On Mission nights you could hear them singing inside to a rollicking jig tune:

> 'Steadily forward march.
> To Jesus we will bring
> Sinners of every kind,
> And He will take them in.
> The rich and poor as well.
> It doesn't matter who.
> Bring them in with all their sin.
> He'll wash them white as snow.'

The beach children came to school grudgingly, trailing up the two miles of flat straight road cut through the rattling dry shingle while the pom-pom guns practised on the head-

51

land and the wind whistled and hissed through the coarse sea-grass and old tins, and the barbed wire made a spitting sound.

They would arrive in school in their plimsolls and their parents' cut-down frocks and trousers. The village children had already formed two lines down the playground when they arrived, with their arms stretched out to touch the shoulders of the pupil in front. The beach children would come across the playground with their sandwich tins and fall into their own line at the side of the playground. They had their own row of desks too at the side of the big classroom that smelt of chalk and wooden board floors and housed the whole school.

'Hew the Bad Tree down!' you would chant, standing beside your desks in your 'standards'.

'Let it live! Mercy cries,' you would rattle out, dividing into two parts. The hymn would end in a unison roar:

> 'Justice cries no!
> Hew the Bad Tree down!'

Then Miss Geddes, the village schoolmistress, would notice that one of the beach boys was fidgeting instead of singing, or that one of the beach girls had forgotten her glasses again. She would come down the aisles between the rows of desks and plant her feet apart wedging them against the iron runners of the desk, dragging the pupil out. There would be a moment's scuffle then a cry as Miss Geddes's ruler came down on their knuckles, or there would be a tussle of gym-shoes against her hard black leather ones, and they would duck out to the front of the class with a whimpering canter, shielding their heads as their mothers had taught them to do as Miss Geddes drove them towards the small room at the side of the class where books and ink and the cane were kept.

There would be a moment's silence and then an abrupt cry from inside:

'Tell me Dad!' And then the beach child would come out tear-stained but smiling: 'Didn't hurt. Old Biffy couldn't hurt a fly.' And when you came to poetry in the morning classes they would recite with the other village children and without a trace of irony in their voices:

52

> '. . . For Nurse had given us sixpence each,
> And we were going down to the beach . . .'

And when you came to the end of the morning and you stood in your lines beside your desks singing:

> 'Gentle Jesus Saviour,
> Do not pass me by,'

you could hear the beach children chanting methodically above the others with stoical reconciliation:

> 'Take me to that land, Jesus.
> Do not pass me by.'

That was your first taste of melancholy, the place of pebbles and withered sea-peas and sickening sorrel and old black tarred huts hung with fishermen's nets, and old black cabins burned out and standing there with just the lamps hanging and the bed springs uncoiling under charred mattresses.

> 'There's a land far far away
> Where 'tis everlasting day'

you would sing when you were dismissed at four and you would run home across the churchyard feeling lightheaded with this promise. The sound of the wind beating against the shingle was in your ears, and its whistling as it blew on the parched sea-peas, and above them came the stoical chant from the beach children's side of the classroom:

> 'Take me to that land, Jesus.
> Do not pass me by.'

Autumn and the rattle of rain on the withdrawing leaves. Heavy yellow leaves stumbling, clopping down with a bang from the trees and roofs and walls. The school year began in September but in October there was time off for picking Victoria plums and Cox's Orange Pippins. But the beach women and their children never went with the village mothers up to the fruit fields. They never left the fruit fields with the wells of their prams loaded with plums, and openly

53

made jam at home, standing the filled pots along their front windowsills to display to the neighbours as the village women did. The beach people's work was digging potatoes or pulling peas and wet thistles that tore their hands and made them stink.

Tourists would stop in the village to photograph the ruined abbey, the Norman church, the old town gates and the smugglers' cottages along the road that had once been the harbour wall before the sea retreated over five hundred years ago down the beach road. The summer visitors never went with their cameras down the dry shingle to where the beach men kept their boats. You would never go down the beach road yourself either. You would go as far as the turning where the beach men stood with their buckets of plaice and dabs and shrimps and then turn away from the sea road down the long lane of chestnuts that led away from the village. The lilac purpling to blackness at its tips. The young copper beeches spreading their bronzing tentacles. The full-faced dandelions. The fields of mustard and the yellow tips of the young oaks. And then the signpost to Happenden and Offenden:

'Take me to that land, Jesus.
Do not pass me by.'

You never went down the beach road. You were afraid of the beach boys slinking round their old railway carriages and throwing stones. As soon as the school was dismissed at four, you would race home to the cottage your mother rented in the village. You would try to persuade her not to come and meet you after school in case she saw the beach boys catching up with you in the playground and turning you upside down till the blood drummed in your head and thrashing you with withies and shouting 'Alleluya' because you sometimes sang the solo in church on Sundays when the congregation went up to receive Holy Communion.

Once your mother had given you a tiny penknife saying it had belonged to your father. It was covered in ivory and had the blurred faded shadow of a tiger painted on one side:

'You mud gid it to us' Brian Helps and John Sands would hold you upside down. 'We'll let you go if you gid it us.' You

54

had given it to them and had walked home feeling that in some way you had affirmed the departure of your father.

But you kept up the pretence of happiness and that you had friends at school though:

'They are good chaps. We are going fishing soon.'

'When, Will?' your mother would ask. 'I want to see you out of that shell and going about with the other village boys. When are you going?'

'Oh, one day soon.' You prayed that she wouldn't come to the school playground at four, but she often did. She was lonely in the village and liked to chat with Miss Geddes.

Your mother used to go up to the fruit fields with the other village women in the summer and autumn, but she was never one of them. Your father had been an accountant in the nearby town. But she was not accepted by the village ladies either. They ran the Brownies and the Dorcas Guild and knitted shawls and binders for Wapping babies or made Coral League bandages for the lepers of Zanzibar.

'Your father was a manly man' your mother would tell you slightly reproachfully and you would feel guilty for preferring to tinkle at the piano or practise your cello or wander alone along the chestnut way, rather than going out with the boys who never came to call for you but would ambush you as you took the turning away from the beach road.

'He was a manly man' your mother would repeat. 'I'm going to have to get you out of that shell and get you playing with the other boys. There must be some nice ones. Who is the one with the nice accent? He must be your type . . .'

'We are going fishing' you would repeat.

'Tomorrow?'

'One day.' And one of those high white promises would descend on you tinged with sadness and you would hear the beach boys singing:

> 'There's a land far far away,
> Where 'tis everlasting day.'

The foxgloves hung heavy in the hedges like gods in pagodas of mauve and pink and white. The chestnut hands stretched out to welcome you. The trees spread round you

55

closer and closer as you neared the place you were always trying to reach where your father went.

Your mother sometimes said she hoped you would become an accountant like your father when you grew up. When she said it the great trees of the lane reared up in front of you and your father was standing by the river weeping beside his shoes. Once when you were seven or so, your godmother had come to stay and when she asked you what you wanted to do when you grew up you had replied:

'I want to commit suicide.'

'Will, dear' your mother had said. 'Be sensible.'

You weren't unhappy at the time when you said it. You simply thought of the great trees of May spreading their leaves out to grasp you and take you into themselves. You saw in the far-off river a kind of fulfilment. It was your destiny to find your father there: the path leading to Happenden and Offenden and your father lying there where the river turned and bent and was brown and still and full and only stirring enough to bear him away. He had fought in the Great War, your mother had told you.

'He was a brave patriotic man.' But you only saw your 'real' father by the river when she spoke. Not that man who was an accountant in the nearby town.

You used to have your cello lessons with a pianist who lived there above a cake shop. Her mother was paralysed down one side and always sat at a table by the window in the room where you were taught, eating custard tart and talking to herself so loudly that Miss Sargent was used to counting:

'One, two, three. Mother dear, please. Seven, eight, nine.'

And you saw the old woman with one eye and one side of her face twisted up into a permanent smile as a victim of the Great War that your mother often spoke about when she said:

'He was a brave man. He fought for his country.'

Once a year Miss Sargent's pupils would give a concert in the local drill-hall. The pupils linked arms and sang:

> 'There are fairies at the bottom of the garden.
> It isn't so very far away.
> You pass the gardener's shed

56

And you just keep straight ahead.
I do so hope they've really come to stay.'

Then girls in mauve dresses would tap-dance in rows:

'If you want to have some fun
When the busy day is done,
Let's all go to the old drill-hall.'

Then you would play a movement of some children's piece
or an aria from an opera that Miss Sargent had arranged for
you. Once it was 'Lead Kindly Light' and you could never
think of that hymn now without smelling Miss Sargent's hot
custard tarts with hundreds-and-thousands sprinkled on them,
or the stained benches and the gas-lighting of the drill-hall
where you performed, or the old lady sitting by the window
with her pulled-up mouth and eye.

'Will there ever be another war?' you asked your mother.

'Soon we shall have to find you a really good teacher' your
mother would reply. 'We shan't stay here for ever. And a
really good school. Time rolls along with a very different per-
spective but everything is quite instructive' she would chuck
you under the chin. 'Your father would have wanted you to
have the best possible education. I know Miss Geddes does
wonders with all those different-aged children. But we can't
blame her if she can't teach you all Latin and maths. We
might even venture as far as London' she looked at you mis-
chievously. 'Would that be fun? It might be worthwhile for
us both.'

It was a hot September day when you went back to school.
The lanes smelt of sweet stinging nettles and hot musty
ditches and the school playground was heavy with dust. In
the school the nurse was going through your heads with a nit-
comb. Several of the beach children were sent home and
came back next day with cloths over their heads reeking of
disinfectant. At lunchtime when you got home your mother
was packing. She told you that the man she rented the cottage from wanted it back and that you would be moving to
London next week. 'Mother has found us a flat in Kennington
... I didn't tell you earlier. I thought I'd keep it as a surprise.'

She had laid the lunch on a piece of newspaper because she had packed the tablecloths. You leaned over it and read a piece about an Adoption Society.

'What does "adoption" mean?' you asked.

'It means bring up a child who is not your own.'

'How can children be not your own?'

'If they come from some other mummy's tummy' your mother replied falteringly. 'Not your own. It means a child you bring up as though it had come from your tummy. Say, if its real parents die or if they can't look after it for some reason.'

'Am I adopted?'

'No, of course you're not.'

'Are you my real mother?'

'Yes, of course I am.' But it came over you mysteriously that she wasn't; that you belonged elsewhere and were in exile here.

You went upstairs to your mother's wardrobe while she was getting the lunch. You gazed at her dresses and at your father's big shoes, the man who had been an accountant and this shy woman, his wife, who would never come into the bedroom when you were undressing; who never came into the bathroom when you were having a bath; who would stand on the other side of the door tapping gently:

'Will dear, have you washed between your groins? . . . Have you been to the dub today? . . . Have you visited "Horace" this morning?'

'Not bored?' she would ask in the evenings when you had had your tea. 'Shall we have a game of draughts? I'm sure you will beat me as you did last time . . .' tilting her head to one side. You had never torn her open and made her stomach bleed. You had never lain in her arms and sucked from her breasts. Once when you had been ill she had tried to make you drink warm milk and water and you had thrown it up, it disgusted you so much, the thin taste of the warm mother's milk. You had not come from her and the man who had been an accountant in the town a few miles away. Your memories were quite other.

A pair of your gloves lay hand by hand, the fingers in rows

in front of you. You remembered how last Christmas your mother had given them to you, and the smell of the new leather and your guilty unease as you opened them and said with pretended surprise and pleasure:

'Gosh! Thank you. Gosh. Thanks tons!'

'What did he die of?' you often asked her, not believing her when she said:

'Food poisoning.'

Food poisoning . . .You were being pushed in a pram that smelt of sour milk and hot India cloth along a narrow path bordered with rushes till you came to the bend in the river where your real father lay among the rushes with his shoes beside him weeping while a little tinkling gramophone buzzed out from the bushes:

'Ninety-nine out of a hundred want to be killed. Why don't you?'

And your mother was standing there angrily chanting: 'Fire, fire burn stick. Stick won't beat dog. Dog won't get over stile and we shan't get home tonight.'

You would sometimes call your mother when she had drawn the curtains at night and said goodnight and gone downstairs:

'Mother, I want you. I want to tell you something' you would call mock-cheerfully. 'Something special.'

And she would come up and kiss you again and you did not say what you wanted to.

'Shall I play you something?' she would ask in the pause. But when she went down and began to play the piano you only saw the rushes and the boat hidden in them which bore your father away like King Arthur to Camelot. Your mother went on playing:

'Mother, I've had enough of that tune. I'd like to go to sleep now.'

'Not afraid of going to London?' she would come back. 'There you'll be able to have a really good cello teacher.' But you were waiting like Isaac, waiting for Abraham to come and lead you away to the river altar as sacrifice.

You crept back to your mother's wardrobe. It smelt of sweat and grease, people's heads and the glandular, sebaceous

59

smell of old hats. You could see a man's suit hanging beside your mother's dresses. You pulled the jacket out. The trousers came out with it and fell across your arms with a jump like a pair of legs leaping out at you, the man there, your adopted father, raising himself up against you for this act of spying on what was not yours. The trouser legs unfolded on you like a rebuke. 'You are not mine. You have no right to exist.'

'We are going to get rid of you' you thought, 'when we move to London.' You looked out over the shredding and shushing autumn trees to the frontier you were never able to pass. 'The exile is real, and from it stems the fantasy of the Kingdom,' Albert Camus has written.

CHAPTER V

But it didn't go, the shadow of a necessary death, even when you got to London.

'If ever there were another war . . . your mother would say, recalling the last time she had lived in London, during the Great War. 'If ever there were another war . . .'

'What would we do?'

'If ever there were another war . . .' she would repeat, pressing her lips together then stopping mysteriously.

Sitting in front of the fire on cold winter evenings in Maisky Street, Kennington, in 1936, she told you about the Great War, the lack of food, the ounce of margarine you got each week tasting of cardboard and sticking to the roof of the mouth; about the long lines of women in sacking aprons and boys' school caps queueing in front of the 'Pussie Butcher' stall in the market for something to make a soup; the big jugs of water cocoa that were handed round in the air-raid shelters at night; and the women in the streets handing out white feathers to the men who would not go to fight.

She told you about the mud and the blood of the trenches in Flanders; the smell of dead horses; the experience of 'going over the top', the sinking of the *Lusitania*; and the Angel of Mons which you pictured shining over the dark foggy streets of Lambeth. She told you about the gas-attacks and her two brothers who were killed by gassing, and the third one who came back with his head held on one side and a fixed smile on his face; and when you went over to see him in the long hospital ward where he was kept, his mouth was smiling but his eyes were still.

> 'What heroes hast thou bred
> Oh England, my country,'
> (you sang in school)
> 'I see the mighty dead
> Pass in line.'

And at night you would lie in bed as the blue night trams clanged their bells, carrying the mighty dead out to places no one knew.

And finally, as though at last she had found some way of communicating with you, got some hold over you at last, your mother would describe the silver and black zeppelins crawling over the streets of London, prying out the houses so that you would call out when she had said goodnight and switched out the bedroom light:

'Mother, I've got something very important to tell you.' And when she came back you had nothing to say except: 'Do you like the colour of the curtains?' or: 'I got a star for arithmetic today.' And she would go through to the sitting room and play hymn tunes to you:

> 'But there's another Country
> I've heard of long ago . . .'

hymn-tunes that only increased your fear of the zeppelins softly perched over the roofs of the flats in Maisky Street, and you would shut your eyes and think of Happenden and Offenden, and the old disused railway-track full of bees and butterflies and foxgloves. The foxgloves peering down at you, you as a child again peering into a spider's web's intricate notation till you saw your father again, his shoes still off, but this time his head cut open, a great gash beside his mouth and his glasses broken in two halves and lying in his shoes; one half in each shoe: 'If ever there should be another war . . .'

'If ever there should be another war' your mother would say as you sat by the fire after school. Tugs' hooters went all day on the river and the smell of fog came in with the smell of hooves and horns being rendered down in the Beefex factory down the road.

At four in the afternoon you could scarcely read the hoarding below you and opposite you in the street:

> 'Boadicea rode a chariot.
> Your pick-me-up is Oxo'

'If ever there were another war . . .' you stared at the advertisement for Heinz baked beans steaming in a dish:

'Would they still be there? All the advertisements?' You had never seen an advertisement in Sussex. 'Get Younger Every Day' . . . you stared out through the fog:

> 'Mummy knows 'cos mummy's cute,
> Rowntrees jellies taste like fruit.'

The yellow fog blurred them away.

You both sat by the fire making a Guy Fawkes. Your mother was knitting its face and stuffing its head with paper and orange peel. You were making the Guy's eyes out of lumps of red plasticine. The smell of burning plasticine came when you thought of the war.

Beyond the yard at the back of the flats where you lived was a row of derelict houses, dark eroded cliffs of them hanging precariously over the street and full of rats and torn flapping wallpaper and broken plaster and joists. Old men slept there and gangs of boys swung in on ropes slung from the street lamps outside. Hotspur Street, Lollard Street and Prince's Road. The houses smelt sour, of jellied eel papers and tomcats and rotting mattresses and the sweet smell of bugs. The wind breathed in and sucked the torn wallpaper to and fro, sucked with lips and cheek and tongue at the tooth-decay in the mouth. Then the mouth would open and you would run away, and the bacon-cutter sound of the red trams slicing round the bend at The Horns public house stopped and the tram ran swaying and crying into the fog, whining as it got up speed in Kennington Road. The long white legs of the Johnny Walker whisky advertisement swung backwards and forwards outside the pub, flashing red and yellow, in and out, over your sitting room. You drew the curtains and ran down Lambeth Walk for some chestnuts to roast.

At one end a stallholder had wrapped herself in a red

blanket and sat there calling into the fog:

> 'Tuppence a pound.
> All sound,'

drinking from a glass of Guinness that rested on the elaborate scrolled till of her stall.

Corsets and long woollen bloomers swung from the rails of stalls. Old glass salt cellars, Mickey Mouse mugs, unmalted vinegar, condiments and bleach, and running down the pavement water drenching an eel that lay beside the great wooden barrel full of a grey writhing mass.

You ran past the tiered stalls laid out with coley and whiting, sprats and whelks; past the rails of strong boys' suits, stiff grey suits with khaki stitching round the pockets and knees; past the rows of ladies' camisoles swinging in the wind; the butcher's stall with piles of smooth brown melts, faggots like horse droppings, pigs' trotters and wiry dried chitterlings squiggling like writing gone wrong, a message of war; and the Herbal Health stall with Kutners Powders, 'Fear, Dread, Sweat and Neuralgia Mixture . . . Disorders of Women treated with One Hundred per cent success . . .' You ran till you came to where the Korn King stood each day in the market. He had spread a Union Jack over his stall and put a brown commode throne on top, and beside it placed a white rubber foot the size of a dog, and stood at the foot's black toenails and the grey hard corn bursting out of its middle toe like a toadstool.

'That corn will soon be dead — no longer here. Put it inside this box' he snapped open a black velvet box and showed three white shiny plugs. 'A lot of people like to take their corns with them to the grave. But this is where I like to put them and keep them, so they needn't, I repeat, they needn't. Because this is where they ought to go.' He tapped his box. Or if it's calluses make your feet sore, I'll put them here alongside the others. And if there's someone you love,' he passed round a picture of an old lady shaking hands with Queen Mary, 'just bring her along here.' He tapped the ground with his stick and placed a packing case beside the stall and helped an old lady up on to his throne. He took out a bottle and a knife and coughed into the fog and fell beside his stall with blood spilling out of his mouth and on to your shoe as you stood there.

'If there were another war . . .' you ran home with blood on your shoe. Your mother was finishing off the Guy Fawkes. You roasted chestnuts in front of the fire:

'If there were another war, what would you do?'

The pigeons stood in rows along the windowsill. The yellow wandering maggot eyes of the evening trams probed the fog. The taste of fog and chimneys was in your mouth. You couldn't see the Beefex advertisement across the street any more.

'Were there any advertisements during the war?' you asked. 'Or did they all get bombed down?'

Your mother took a piece of paper and rolled it into two long thin pencils: 'That much butter we had. And that much coconut butter each week. And it tasted like dirty clothes. And the bombings! The zeppelins! They came over every night and we ran into the shelters and sang very loudly: "Keep the Home Fires Burning, for the Boys will soon be Home". But of course they never did come home, except for a few like Uncle George.'

Your Uncle George in the hospital never spoke. He only held his head on one side and rhymed whatever you said, wearing a college blazer and a straw hat as though he were going boating, or like a sunny man on a pier, winking and rhyming and endlessly taking off his hat and putting it on again.

There was another ex-soldier who sat on a kitchen chair changing the tram-points at The Horns, pulling at a metal bar with his one arm. 'If there were another war, what would we do?' you continued to ask, sitting by the fire. The coal shifted against the bars of the grate with a waiting, listening sound. You waited attentively, thinking of the men of Ypres with glass eyes and wooden legs and hollow metal arms like gas pokers, and crutches with black padded leather tops that thrust in and out at you like wicked hips as they limped along in front of you in the street; seeing the men in invalid carriages pulling and pushing at their long handles and

65

pumping themselves down Maisky Street; looking out of the window at the trams on chains being led blindly like the wounded and the gassed; the blue night trams that crept secretly past at three in the morning whispering 'Put out your dead.'

'So what would you do?'

'And they put out long lists of the dead and the wounded every day, pinning them at the street corners, and a woman was standing there crying at the lists and clutching a wooden pram with red roses and green butterflies painted down its sides, rocking it up and down by its one broken handle as she cried, and the zeppelins were out again. The Great War was so terrible.'

'So what would you do if there was another?'

Your mother shook her head, said nothing. You prompted her:

'Would you kill us both?'

'Will dear!'

You ran into the kitchen and switched the gas-tap up: 'Pooh! It smells of biff.'

'Will dear!'

'Or put us in the Ideal Boiler?' you shouted, staring at the big capital letters over the kitchen stove: 'IDEAL BOILER'. 'Ideal, but too small. You'd have to shrink us first with yellow soap. But we could get into the fire in the sitting room in turns.'

'Will dear! The Guy's eyes are ready to be stuck in.'

After that your mother never said 'If there were another.'

'Have you done any practising today?' she changed the subject. You shook your head. You would shiver when you played your bottom C like the zeppelins coming over. 'Will dear, there must be little gnomes who sleep until we start working. Then they come into our room and start to worry and tease us. Sometimes, I expect, it's hard to keep your mind on what you are playing, but you must learn to ignore the gnomes. I'm sure it'll prove profitable in the end.'

Your mother was a coward. She had failed you. You took to walking home from school past the Imperial War Museum to see the gun-carriages and the hooded waggons thinking of

66

the blinds down, the door knockers wrapped, the horses with bandaged eyes and padded hooves stalking blindfold through the empty night streets.

A woman came to the door one day. She asked for money and said the King was dead. She stood there holding *Old Moore's Almanac* and a bundle of firewood, driftwood that the men picked up at night from Lambeth Steps, always after dark because driftwood belonged to the King.

But the King was dead and you stood in a long queue in the fog over Vauxhall Bridge and down Kennington Lane to walk past his bier. As a tram roared and rocked over the points you heard someone crying:

'They're taking him away.'

It was Christmas. Your grandparents came. Gran was sitting by the fire when you got in from school. She toasted you some bread and spread it thickly with jam and you sat on the arm of her chair eating and plunging your hands into her thick hair:

'It's all grey underneath' you said. 'Soon it'll all be grey and then you'll be dead.'

'Not for a long time yet' she replied cheerfully making more toast. It was Christmas and you were rehearsing a Nativity play about the Three Kings for your grandparents. Your mother was one king. The girl next door was another, and you were the third. Your grandmother played the piano and dressed you in a gold cape and a hat on to which she had stuck some jelly sweets for jewels. The three Kings went down into the yard and climbed the iron fire-escape steps to the flat singing 'We Three Kings of Orient Are' while your grandparents waited in the sitting room for the play to begin.

' "Gold I bring to crown him again" ' you sang, then shouted suddenly: 'Well, if these kings were so rich, why didn't they take Jesus home with them to their palaces?' Your neck was very red. You felt hot and cold and began to scream: 'I don't see why we have to go on and on about dead kings.'

Gran put you to bed and peeled an orange for you and told you a story:

'So the cats all went in at one door and the mice all went

in at another. They had their own entrance further up, you see.'

'Yes but how many doors away?'

'Six.'

'Why only six?' you screamed.

' "Once in Royal David's City" ' she began to sing. When she came to the end:

> ' "And He leads his children on
>   To the place where He is gone" '

you screamed again. She took your toy rabbit down from the mantelpiece: 'Mrs Rabbage says she's very tired today. She went to Kennington Park yesterday and ate so many dandelion leaves that her jaws ache now and she just wants to go to sleep and rest her ears.'

She put Mrs Rabbage on the bed beside you. You threw her out:

'She's only a doll. She's dead. They're all dead.' You were taken away to Liverpool Road Isolation Hospital with a mask over your face. Next week they all came to see you. You sat there and refused to look at the Christmas presents they had bought for you: an orange, a bath cube, *The Black Arrow*, a red wooden apple that opened and had chocolate pen-nibs inside. The ward Sister stood there in a long black dress with silver stars down it and told them to bring your clothes and get you dressed. You cried all the way home from Islington on the No. 33 tram, banging your feet agains the wooden sides of the tram seats till a woman with torn ear-lobes turned round:

'I'd twank him one, if he was one of mine.'

'He's been ill' your mother apologised. You cried again when you turned the corner of Maisky Street and saw through the fog the hoarding displaying huge red beans in a steaming dish, and the Oxo twins swooning over beef-extract, and the top of the No. 33 tram rocking and swinging round the bend by The Horns. 'And what about the war?'

'There won't be another war we hope' your mother tried to reassure you.

You were taken to the Pantomime, 'Puss in Boots', and you

kept asking when the story was going to begin. A clown with a white melancholy face came on to the stage and sang:

'I don't want to go to bed. I don't want to go to bed. Oh me! Oh my! I don't want to go to bed.'

You didn't want to go to bed. You lay in the dark and called your mother to leave the door open and play the piano. You could hear the blue night trams clanging 'Put out your dead'. You called out and your grandmother came and sang to you:

' "Suffer the Little Children
And let them come unto Me".'

Suffer meant suffocate. You saw the suffocated children being brought to Christ. Rows of children hung by silken cords like the stoats you had sometimes seen in the country, in the woods. There won't be another war . . .

Gran bought you a torch and you made a film projector out of a shoe box with the torch shining behind it. You made some cocoa and drew the curtains of your bedroom and invited the grown-ups and the girl next door to come in to a film show called 'Do not despair until death'. The film was about Franco and Adolph Hitler. You had cut out photographs of them in uniform saluting and stuck pictures of Fyffes' bananas on their shoulders for arms. Only the film didn't move fast enough and the audience grew bored and started to drink the jug of cocoa you had put under the bed for the interval, and the night grew in Maisky Street and the trams howled.

At three in the afternoon the electric lights in the school classroom had a ring of fog round them and outside the window the world hung suspended like yellow tripe. The smell of menthol and 'Owbridge's Lung Tonic' and the creosote of 'Famel Syrup' hung round the classroom. You took turns to read aloud from *The Lancers of Lynwood*. As you read, the boy next to you, Edward Rutt, stabbed his compasses between each of your outspread fingers, jabbing the compass points into the desk in the spaces between them. He had warts on his hands and invited you home to tea over his father's shop. You went there. Over the shop-window was written: 'Edward Rutt. Inexpensive Funerals. Our Horses Go Any Distance.' When you read it and saw the black horses pawing in the yard behind and a huge black pall with initials embroidered in silver on each corner standing in the shop, and the photograph of men in black in front of the cortege holding banners swathed in black, you said that your mother would be expecting you home at once; said you had forgotten to tell her you were going out to tea. 'We're a quiet family. We don't go out much.' And you could see John Rutt's mother in the little parlour at the back preparing tea behind the shop full of tombstones and photographs of horses drawing black hearses out to the cemetery.

'Will dear' your mother said when you got in, 'we ought always to think of the feelings of the people we mix with. This may sometimes prove a little hard but I'm sure in the long run we'll find it to be worthwhile. All right?' She put her head on one side and smiled at you: 'All right?'

'Cor' said your grandfather, 'I wouldn't have missed those iced-cakes for the world.'

'I would' said your grandmother. 'I hate funerals. I want to be buried with cheerful music and flap-jacks for tea. I've had a lovely life.' Then they went back home to Sussex. You thought of Happenden and Offenden often now.

It was 1937 and you were coming home from your cello lesson on the tram. The chain at the driver's end clanked harder and harder against the tram's metal side as it got up speed along the Kennington Road, singing higher and higher up the scale and into the dark.

'All tickets please' the conductor came down the tram banging his ticket rack against the sides of the seat and flicking through his piles of unpunched tickets. The woman on the seat next to you wore gym-shoes and a sacking apron and had a cabbage leaf over a swollen vein on her leg like blue chitterlings against the bare white of her flesh. When the conductor came to take her fare she didn't move. There was foam at the corners of her mouth and her head was tilted up against the notice above her: 'No spitting. Penalty Forty Shillings.'

'If there were another war . . .' if her head jerked down

70

there would be. If she spoke there wouldn't be. She sat there rigidly. You stepped over her to get out at The Horns. If anyone got on there would be. If there was no one at the stop there wouldn't be. If you met a man as you turned the corner into Maisky Street there would be. You began to play a game of 'is' and 'isn't'. It is, something in the street would say. Or it isn't, someone would reply. You would ask your mother to play the piano. If she said 'All right' it isn't. If she said 'Just let me take off my pinafore first,' it is. It is. It isn't. You looked out of the window. The lamplighter was putting his ladder against the lamp-post. If he comes up to the window, if he peers in, then it is. He lifts the window and climbs into your bedroom: 'I have come from Wappenden to take you back.'

Your mother went to the oilman's shop and bought you night-lights. There were brooms and mops hanging from the chandler's ceiling, kettles and rat-traps, mouse-traps, fly-papers and fly-swats hanging from the dark rafters, and blue sacks of salt in the corners and brown sacks of beans and sugar. If the lady asked for beans, it is. If she asked for sugar then it isn't. At the counter they were talking about the bombing of Barcelona. On the floor there was a gob of phlegm streaked with blood. As you passed the derelict houses in Hotspur and Lollard Street you saw them like the bombed houses of Barcelona and Madrid.

'Will, what about your practising?' your mother asked when you got in with the night-lights. You tried to practise but you kept hearing the beach boys chanting with stoic fortitude at the end of the morning:

'Oh Master when my last end is come,
Bid angels bear my body home
To God which is its Maker.
Then standing in that glorious place . . .'

The wind whistled over the shingle and barbed wire and sea-peas. Your mind turned you away from the beach road and up into the tunnelled land to Happenden. The river had dead leaves floating on it. Your father beckoned.

Your mother lit your night-light. 'Leave the door open a

71

bit. Leave the light on in the hall . . . Mother' you would call her a few moments later, 'I've got a secret I want to tell you.' And she would come back so that you could smell her supper cooking as she stood in the doorway of your room.

'What is it?' she tried to sound excited.

'The one remaining lion on the salt-cellar's legs has got a name. Guess what it is.'

'Leo?'

'No. You've got to guess its name while I count up to twenty.' And you would lie there counting very slowly while your mother stood in the door of your room clicking the knob while supper smells came from the kitchen and you thought: 'If she guesses, it isn't.'

'Absalom? Peter? Dick?' she clicked the door knob.

A few days ago when you had come in from school and switched the gas-burner on to boil a kettle for tea you had heard a faint clicking sound and heard a tinkling of metal against metal and saw that you had left the silver salt-cellar on the gas-burners and that three of its lions' legs had melted off, and fallen onto the hot-plate under the stove. You hid the awry legless salt-cellar and your mother had complained for a week about its disappearance. Finally you climbed into her bed late one night just as she was falling asleep and confessed what you had done. You had expected her to say:

'Will dear, we ought to try and be more careful with other people's property. That was a present from your father.' But she didn't. Instead she yawned: 'I never did like that salt-cellar. I always thought it was silly with those lions' legs at the corners. Who wants lions' legs sticking at the corner of a salt-cellar? And anyway, the inside was rough and set my teeth on edge. And an egg-cup is much more useful for salt.' Was that an is or an isn't?

She went on standing in your bedroom door trying to guess the name of the one remaining leg. 'My supper's burning' she interrupted her guesses. 'I'll go and think it over while I eat.'

'What are you having?'

'A fried egg like you had.'

'Which do you like better, fried or boiled?' Boiled. It was.

72

'Which would you rather, mutton with wobbly fat hanging round it or pigs' trotters?'

'Mutton. I think.' It wasn't.

And so it would go on until at last she went and the rattle and clanking of trams came back in the dark, and gangs of women came down the street roaring and fighting drunkenly turning round the bend where their men had gone and would not come back.

And the tram conductor turning the seats round at the end of the run found the woman with the cabbage leaf over her veins still sitting there with her head lifted to the 'No spitting' sign. A fly was walking over her eyeball. Foam was at the corners of her mouth, and you ran into the kitchen where your mother was sopping up egg-yolk with dry bread:

'If Franco wins ... If Mr Hitler invaded Czechoslovakia ...?' And when the Spanish Republic fell and German troops entered Prague in March 1939 your mother still said:

'There won't be another war. Mr Chamberlain has been to Munich and seen to that.'

But the night sounds still came to you and you turned and saw, half-hidden by the curtains, two khaki gas-masks that you had to try on. They smelt powdery, of vanilla and chalk, and had glass eyeholes you had to soap so that they would not steam over with your breath during the longest gas-attacks.

September the third and you went to the tall white gleaming Lutyens church of St Anselm at Kennington Cross and sang: 'Oh God our Help in Ages Past'. Then the organ roared out:

'Time like an Everlasting Stream
Bears all its Sons away.'

It is. It is. It is. You walked out into the sunshine with your mother. An animal curiosity came over you. You wanted to know what the world looked like now that you were at war again.

CHAPTER VI

September the third was a hot white misty day with an iso-lated pale sun swinging round the mucous sky. A man stood on the rusty fire-escape down the backs of the flats pouring distilled water on to the black and silver honeycombs of an accumulator. A woman on the landing above was letting water drop from her mangling down into the yard below. It came drip-crackle-drip behind the voice of Neville Chamberlain declaring war on Germany. You leaned over the railings into the yard beneath. Some boys below were standing round a man who had collapsed on the tarmac. Had war started already?

The siren went, stretching from its bass ground under the streets and rising slowly to a high female cry. It dropped again then rose, like a Big Dipper at a fair-ground swooping down and round and up and taking your stomach with it as it rose and fell.

You ran down to the shelter that had been dug in the yard and sat face-to-face in the dark on the wooden benches clutching your gas-masks while an Air-Raid Warden tried to get you to join in the singing: 'Underneath the Spreading Chestnut Tree.' A girl got up and tap-danced down the plank-floor between the benches singing:

> ' "When you're browned off just say it's
>   tickety-boo,
>   For tickety-boo means everything's going to
>   be fine." '

You waited for the dark pall over the city, the sleek planes hovering over the streets, the trams roaring 'Put out your dead'.

'He was a brave man, your father was' your mother was saying. 'He would be doing his bit now. Try to join in the singing:

' "Thumbs up, tickety-boo, tickety-boo".' But you sat there refusing to join in. At Happenden the summer would be drying out, and the river slow and still and calling out to you, and you were embarrassed by the intrusion of this accountant who had died of food-poisoning.

The all-clear went and you came out of the shelter. A tram clattered round the bend at The Horns. The smell of fish-and-chips came from the Perfecto Fish Caterer; the smell of ginger from Steng's the spice-merchant on Kennington Green; and a notice hung in the advertisement-case outside the tobacconist's:

'Girls! Do you want to earn some pocket money for Christmas? Why not join the chorus of Mother Goose in this year's pantomime at the Camberwell Palace?' Nothing had changed. You went home and had bacon and fried bread for dinner. Afterwards you wandered round again to see what the world looked like now that the cataclysm had happened.

'Mummy knows 'cos Mummy's cute
Rowntrees jellies taste like fruit'

still hung on the wall on the other side of Maisky Street. A man on a ladder was pasting up a new one. You watched the words coming out of the paste pot and paper one by one:

'Kettle boiling, tea in pot.
This reviver beats the lot.'

'Still the same. Nothing's happened yet.' You went home shaking your head.

'What?' your mother asked.

' "Zam-Buk. Rub it in", and "Ouch my poor feet".' No great change yet. No cataclysm under the white sky.

You wandered past The Horns to the Oval and took off your shoes and socks and stood in the paddling pool pressing your toes into the mud and dead leaves on its bottom. Everything was quiet. A woman with a baby on her arm came up to you and stroked your wrists and asked for money. You ran away and she followed you with the baby, carrying the wet socks you had left behind. You could see her following you and see the dark drips the wet socks made in the dry autumn plane-seed dust on the pavement. The woman with the baby hung outside the front door of your flat till your mother gave her money and food, and she sat on the glittering stone public stairs eating and dipping her handkerchief into her tea and letting the baby sup from it.

And in spite of the war, the Salvation Army still came down the road as usual that Sunday to their afternoon Witness Meeting singing 'Good Times Coming'. And boys followed them as usual chanting:

> 'Salvation Army
> All gone barmy.'

You sat in a tent you had made from a blanket pinned out over the fire-escape railings chanting:

> 'Here comes the Boys' Brigade
> All smothered in marmalade.'

'My big son is growing callous and silly about the war' your mother complained as you sat there mechanically chanting all afternoon. 'He certainly doesn't seem at all bothered about the Germans.'

The day grew hotter. Someone had opened the stop-cock in the yard, and you took turns, standing round in your bathing costumes, to stand under the cool spout of water that splashed over the tarmac. Only a few children were left in Maisky Street. Most had been evacuated to Kent and Sussex.

'Would you like to go and stay with Gran and Gramp till nasty Mr Hitler is beaten?' your mother asked. 'Of course it would mean giving up your cello for the duration.' You had just started going up into the first position and you had joined a small children's orchestra and played movements by Purcell and bits of Handel's 'Water Music'. You shook your head. The streets were quiet.

Your mother got a job in a paper factory and sent you out

each morning after she had gone out with a shilling to the 'Cash-and-Carry' that had been set up at the end of Kennington Lane. It was a shop with bare scrubbed tables and chairs down the middle where old men sat coughing over their newspapers. You would take a pudding-basin with you and get it filled with mince or cottage pie and carry it home for your evening meal, and then practise.

Or you went to the 'Leopard' Dining-Rooms in Camberwell New Road and sat in one of the wooden pews eating pie-and-mash, pie-and-peas or jellied pigs' trotters. You started attending the South-East London Emergency School and got a good music teacher who actually played the cello. You studied your first sonata. It had a long slow sad falling second movement and your teacher introduced you to vibrato and you found you could produce a beautiful tone.

January came and there was still no sign of war. Rationing started and you went for your mother to the old Music Hall that had been turned into the Food Office and got your ration-books, queueing for two hours in the burst red upholstered seats of the stalls while women on the stage sat at long trestle tables by small electric fires that scorched the wood of the tables and singed the hair on their bare legs.

They sat there with blunt stubs of pencils cancelling, cutting and stamping ration books and making out identity cards, snipping at pages not yet in use, pasting in special concessions for babies and children, blocking out boxes and cancelling points. They worked in the dim light of the great glass chandelier in the centre of the Music Hall and as you waited you took in the chipped gilt fronts of the boxes and the old red torn seating and the whitewashed steps running up to a gallery hanging so steeply it looked as though it were going to topple down on you. You had never been in the theatre before except for that melancholic 'Puss in Boots', and you used to enjoy going to the Food Office for your mother and sitting in the dim light among the empty seats still full of lingering expectation. You would picture the lights lowered and the dusty red and silver curtains swaying with the weight and mystery of all that lay behind them, the pelt of red riding up while you sat in the orchestra pit and your cello suddenly rose towering up over the violins as the curtain swayed and lifted. You went home and practised. You resolved to become a famous performer and play your slow movements to the gilt boxes and the red plush stalls and the packed and toppling gallery.

February and a tense white cold, and the frost along the roofs still white at four in the afternoon. The pigeons' whirr as they strutted into the butcher's shop and he drove them out with a meat skewer and came back in with one impaled and kicked it into a corner. The grey buildings looming dark against the white sky. Sometimes a yellow sun wobbling for a moment in the fog and then gone. The smell of biscuits came from the factory at the Elephant and Castle. The smell of gas and jam and pickles. For your birthday your mother gave you a street map of London and you would pore over it all day, turning bends 'And this is where the jam smell is so strong. And this is where you can smell the beer from the brewery.'

The smell of gas and pickles. The smell of the public sparkling stairs leading up to your flat. The smell of electricity from the Oval underground station. The smell of newsprint and pencil wood inside Alming's Bazaar. Pencil sharpeners, Japanese tea-sets, pink celluloid chairs and tables; and opposite, The Horns, and the shadow of men inside the frosted glass with Allsops Ales written into it. The huge drays with four horses and a man in oilskin covers sitting in a high seat up in front and the four horses stamping and letting their breath curl out into the cold winter air like trumpet blasts. . . You still waited for the cataclysm, but you no longer needed a night-light at night. And you practised two hours every day thinking of the old Music Hall and your vibrato reaching to the top of the leaning toppling gallery.

March and people began talking about the phoney war and your mother received a letter from the Royal Academy asking you to go for a scholarship audition. You played to a tall man with a shock of white hair. He listened in silence while you played your sonata, then he examined your instrument:

'It is too small for you now, and your tone is poor. And

that slow movement is too difficult. We shall have to begin at the beginning again. You don't allow your bow to sink into the strings enough. You play on the top of your strings. Laugh in that last movement and keep the six-eight rhythm going happily. Instead of clenching your teeth and your jaw when you go into the second position, open your mouth and relax. Now good. Laugh. Dance it.'

You didn't get the scholarship, but you got a Junior Exhibition and went up to the Academy every Tuesday morning for lessons, and worked at Piatti studies, for weeks nothing but crossing from one string to another, or keeping the bow parallel with the bridge. For weeks nothing but simple fughettas in the first position. For weeks nothing but scales and arpeggios, concentrating on intonation.

Summer came and France fell and you came home crying down the street:

'Pétain is a swine. Laval is a swine.'

'They will not come' your mother said quietly after Dunkerque. 'We will not let them.' The Battle of Britain took place and you waited. Summer and you longed to be walking along the lane to Happenden. Or to go down to Sussex and see your grandparents. But your mother patriotically said you must have holidays at home, a government campaign, and you obeyed and went together and sat in Kennington Park listening to the Band. Or you went swimming at Manor Baths in the Walworth Road or you took the boat from Lambeth Pier down to Greenwich and ate ices in Greenwich Park or you went to Peter Pan's Pool at Catford and drove your mother round the lake in a small electric boat shaped like a swan. Then in September you went back to school. Evacuees had come trickling back from Kent and Sussex. Others had been sent off to Wales. Your lessons at the Academy started again:

'Let's make that phrase curved not angular . . . Too much. Too generous. And you are using too much bow. That's better. That's lovely. Now bring your bow right back to the nut . . .'

You always remembered that lesson because that night you dreamed you were climbing up your cello bow and each time you reached the acacia tree growing on the top, the flowers on the tree would be blown off by a great crashing wind. You tried to wake but the dream came again. Great metal cylinders were crashing out of the top of your bow. Your mother was shaking you:

'Will, we must go downstairs and shelter.' You took a blanket each, and crossed the yard. There was a scream like a car skidding, like brakes being jammed suddenly on, rubber screaming. Then came the explosion. Then an extraordinary silence before the guns in Kennington Park started up again: 'Ah. Ah. Ah.'

The shelter in the yard was full. You ran back across the yard to the flats. The searchlights were doing sword-fights in the sky. One caught a tiny white cross up there. Shrapnel was falling. You ran into the basement where the dustbins were kept. Mrs Ems who lived next door to you was rocking backwards and forwards:

'Here they come. Here we are at last. They're coming. You should of sent that child of yourn away.'

You could hear the drone of planes and the whining screams of bombs and the anti-aircraft guns high tank-tanking in the sky, a sound as though great metal dustbins were being beaten above you. In a lull you lay down by the dustbins and slept and dreamed you were inside an egg and the top was being cracked open and torn off and you woke when a bomb came down very near and sucked the windows of the basement in then out and the door burst open.

When the all-clear went, you went out into the street. It was a cold frosty night, the kind in which you can feel the world's breath and the ends of the earth seem to reach you. But the sky was red and there was a smell of plaster and rubble and brick-dust. Charred strands of paper floated into your mouth and nose.

'They got the paper factory in Gracie Street' someone shouted. 'It's all that paper going up.'

'Abominable!' you said. You didn't often try to joke with your mother.

In the morning you went down the road to school. Alming's Bazaar had lost its windows but the shopkeeper was

80

still selling india-rubbers and magic paintbooks, Kutflem and Winter Mixture. The skittering of footballs came from the yards. The skuttering of pigeons scraping and clattering on the roofs. There was a smell of plaster and tomcats from damp gutted houses. Hotspur Street had been opened up after a hundred years and it was letting out the sweet smell of rats and damp into the early morning. But when you heard the trams coming round the bend at The Horns now, it was a welcome sound. It simply meant that the raid was over, and you were determined to stay alive. You had only a local fear. It wasn't invasive. It didn't invade your inner space as the First World War had done. The sounds outside were like rock cracking, cloth splitting, splitting silk in the sky. And you were alive and forgot the pumping sound of invalid carriages coming in long dark columns down the street, and the woman with foam at her mouth and a fly walking over her eyeball, and the black zeppelins sneaking like cats between the roofs of the city.

'Is this as bad as the Great War?' you asked your mother again and again, and she would say:

'Much worse,' staring at you as if thinking how insensitive children were to the horrors of war. 'However, I'm glad you're still cheerful. We want you all to stay cheerful. It's good that you should. And your music absorbs you so much these days.'

After the first raid you took your bedding down to the Oval underground station at night. Bunks lined the platforms.

'Bags the top bunk' you cried, staring at the posters on the tube tunnel walls: 'Be like Dad. Keep Mum.' . . . 'Careless Talk Costs Lives' and the finger of an airman pointing at you wherever you stood: 'You can help me build a gun.' 'Bags the top bunk!' you scrambled onto a free bunk and dumped your bedding. A big fat woman in a black velvet hat bore down on you:

'The effing cheek! Get off that! You're not a regular.' So you sat down on the 'Try your weight' scales and made your bed up beside it, while your mother had the Fry's Chocolate Cream machine. You slept on and off until the sound of the all-clear came, the rich sleek satisfied 'Ah-Ah', and the cheerful rumbling sound of the all-night trams running again.

If you had been very frightened you would whisper to your mother: 'Prickly Pears'. If the bomb fell further away you would sing out 'Only apples'.

'Yes, it was only apples that time,' your mother would agree.

Every evening in the tube station had its own ritual. On Mondays you would play 'Which would you rather?' inventing two traumatic things to do. 'Which would you rather, eat aspirins made into soup or chew clinker?' On Tuesdays you would play 'Animal, Vegetable or Mineral'. On Wednesdays you would go to the Oval via Almings Bazaar and buy sweets and Comic Cuts and Film Fun. On Fridays when you got there your mother had been paid and she would pull out of her bag a banana or an orange or a piece of chocolate she had got in her canteen, a Mars bar she cut carefully into six thin slices and you would eat a slice each hour, dissolving the sweetness slowly in your mouth.

One week she would buy you a piece of new music to play. Once it was Bach's 'Bist Du bei Mir' arranged for cello and piano. And you rushed home next morning to play it together. Once it was a map of Sussex and you lay there looking at it, following the road to Happenden till the last train had gone through and your mother pulled out a packet of bread with stewed apple on it, 'Our nightly snackerel' she would call it, and you ate and fell asleep not hearing the beach boys singing stoically at the end of the school morning but the sounds of people down the platform singing 'There'll Come Another Day'.

Your mother was calling you to breakfast when you got back from the tube station one morning. She was asking you to lay the table. You laid nutcrackers and a tea strainer in her place and a fish-slice and a tin-opener in your own. She put a fried egg down in front of you. You threw it in the air and caught it on the fish-slice. You shovelled tomato into your mouth with a tin-opener. She sat down and struggled with her nutcrackers and tea strainer. Egg splashed on the table.

You both laughed. 'I transcend the war' you would have run off to school crying if you had known the word. You passed the shops with their boarded-up windows with a tiny glass pane in the front that you could peer through and the cheerful notices 'Business as Usual'. Your war was to come much later.

You began to play well: 'Try to get that phrase folded back nicely out of its shell. Lovely. Good. Let's go. Think of it first before you play it. Let your fingers not your body play. Shoulder down. You're flat there. Less fluff on that G string. Try a single bow on that phrase and sing it. Let's go. Let's try to get it. Good. Good. Lovely.'

And with these words carried with you, you would leave your lesson. Once in your elation you wandered down through Baker Street and along Oxford Street and Regent Street to Trafalgar Square to the National Gallery and paid a shilling for a lunchtime concert. It was Myra Hess playing Bach's Chorale Prelude 'Sanctify Us' and as you heard the bass theme penetrating urgently the measured serenity of the right hand's pondering delicate phrases you felt a sudden excitement. A sudden high white conviction that you too could enter the kingdom of beauty. You could never again hear that Chorale played without smelling the cool varnish smell of the National Gallery and seeing the gilt wicker chairs set in rows and remembering the noise of the nights and a kitchen dresser still standing against a fragment of bombed wall with its china hanging in rows. You could never hear the Bach Chorale again without seeing the toothbrush still hanging against the wall of a bombed bathroom and the bath half-toppling over into the rubble beneath and seeing these and feeling that there was a world reserved and untouched by anything that man could do.

After that first recital you wandered up to Augener's in Marlborough Street and bought a copy of the Chorale. The air was suddenly full and sweet like a seashore. You sat in Lyons in Whitehall drinking tea, smelling the yellow fish at the counter and reading the music and growing excited again by the way the bass line spoke through the serene pattern of the treble, stood guardian over the rhythmic pattern of

83

question and answer in the right hand. You walked home hearing the bass line riding triumphantly up over the wounded city. For the first time you were driven in your playing not by nostalgia but by a state of war, and a Kingdom over against it that you would one day enter and explore . . . 'Relax your right arm. Let it fall. Drop heavily on to your bow as though you were stepping down the last steps of a steep ladder and into a boat to carry you away . . .'

You would go to lunchtime concerts after every cello lesson then walk up to Augener's and buy scores. Once you bought the St John Passion and were excited when after the denial of Christ — 'Let Him be crucified' — the chorus, instead of flagellation and weeping and *grincement de dents*, bursts out into 'Thy Name Oh Lord is Shining'. A burst of joy in place of terror and anguish and remorse. A structure of hope and forgiveness and surprise. That is how you wanted to play.

In June 1944 you started learning Beethoven's Sonata No. 4 in G. 'Your left thumb is lazy. It too has to play. Think of your thumb as a popper or a press stud that has to close an opening. Don't push the bow along like an engine. Let it fly. Let it lead your hand lightly along the beautiful legato. And that phrase must have a beginning and a middle and an ending. You are still not bringing it to an end . . .' You rushed home to practise. That summer night the first flying bomb came over. A strange lumbering sound like a clumsy lawn-mower trundling over the sky. Then the uncouth noise stopped. There was a moment's silence, then as you stood at the window watching the black machine hanging there silently in the sky with a great red bum at the end of it, it dropped suddenly with a crash and another came over and cut out and you waited for the explosion. You could hear the nurses screaming in the Nurses' Home down the road under the rubble. Soon they gave up sounding the alarm when flying bombs came over. People gave up taking cover when the grinding sound started in the sky. At first just a faint mowing sound like beer rising in a glass or the sea at low tide tickling with its low hum at the edge of the beach. Then the heavy clumsy bungling lawn-mower sound. The trundling sound. Then silence as its engine cut off.

You would be queueing for fish paste or sausages when it came.

'Been celebrating, have you?' the butcher was asking the woman in front of you when she dropped her purse.

'Very quietly. My son came home on leave last night.'

'I bet he gave you a strong one .'

'A Mackeson's. That's all. Are the sausages pork or beef today?'

'One leg's beef and one leg's pork. And I can let you have half a pound. But I've got some nice mince today. You could make a nice shepherd's pie. The kind that don't repeat on you when you get out into the open air.'

Then you heard the sound. The butcher went on serving till its engine cut off. 'Here it comes.' Two women climbed under his chopping bench. The rest just moved inside the shop and waited.

'That one must have come down Clapham way.'

When your turn came, the sausages and the mince had all gone and all you could get for supper was a tub of fish-paste. Another one came over as you turned into Maisky Street. Mrs Ems stood at her door beckoning you in. You both sat down under her table. There was a moment's silence and then a winding decline. You sat among broken glass.

'They say there's even worse to come' Mrs Ems began. 'Rockets and a Channel tunnel . . . Doreen didn't take her mac today and it's going to rain. I told her to take mine. Hers is all split under the arms she's putting on weight so with all this bread and syrup.' She started sweeping up the glass.

When you went out someone told you that it was the paper factory again where your mother worked. You got there in time to see her carried off on a stretcher with a mac over her. Overalls and stockings and hats and sandwich tins were scattered over the road. The A.R.P. men were digging. Your mother was whimpering as they straightened her on the stretcher. You went to South Lambeth Hospital to visit her. She was in traction with a great cut over her eye and they were still taking metal and glass out of her legs and arms.

'You must take cover when anything cuts out' she told

85

you. 'But it didn't hurt half so much when they first brought me' she kept repeating through dry peeling lips. Her speech was slurred with thirst but the feeding cup was too heavy for her to lift to her lips. And the sky was bone white.

The classes at the Emergency School had been disbanded because of the risk of a direct hit. You sometimes went to school though and sat all day in the staff cloakrooms in the basement singing 'Jerusalem' or 'See where the beacon fires of faith, Fling glory to guide us.' Or you played charades or Twenty Questions. You stopped going there and spent your day practising or going to concerts or going to visit your mother in hospital. Men stood at the windows in turkish towel dressing gowns. The blankets on the beds were hot and red. 'But we are winning' you would tell your mother. 'The war is nearly over.'

'Is Mrs Ems looking after you all right?' your mother would ask. Her body seemed small and perilous beside the big white cups of tea and the toothmug and toothbrush. As though they were aimed at her, were making war on her along with the heavy chipped black iron traction frame.

You went to another lunchtime concert at the National Gallery. Camberwell tram depot had been hit and so you had to walk. It was hot and the streets smelt of glue and boiling plasticine, parched rubber, hot jam, and burning corset bones still smoking after a fire. But you were a musician. You played over this smell of war, this drought, this death.

'The tone must not be laid on the passage but produced from within the strings. That's muffled. That's blurred. You haven't really felt that lovely Andante. Let it come. It's still confused. Vacant. Gaping. Let your bow and your shoulder clear it up. Good.'

An ice-cart went past trickling water from its rear on to the dry streets. A fire of wooden joists was burning, the floors of bombed houses. Someone had fed serge on to the fire. A foul stench came up. You were riding along on the top of a roofless tram going to the National Gallery.

The Griller Quartet was playing. They wore R.A.F. uniforms and played the Mozart in D minor, K.456. You could never hear it again without remembering when you were fifteen and Happenden was taken away from you and re-placed by a simple Chorale Prelude or a joyful quartet.

Once or twice in the sixties you had been to hear the children of the Yehudi Menuhin School play. Children who played sublimely with great ease and joy and freshness. They once played the Brahms Sextet in B. It was a new tone range that child art gave. Ripe apricots. Sunshine. Disinterested-ness. Nothing coming between them and their instruments and the music. A careful passionate placement of sounds without knowingness or cunningness or conscious sensuality. The open and transparent. The innocent seeing eye getting in first before the intellect had placed the sounds or imposed pattern on them. Receiving things whole without too much interpretation. 'The ability to be in uncertainties, mysteries, doubts, without any irritable reaching after fact and reason.' The innocent eye, seeing everything for the first time new and clear. Sympathies that sprang from nothing but the row of unfolding notes. The instrument as a tin-opener . . . When you heard the children playing you thought for a moment that you must have played like that when you were first given a Beethoven Sonata or a movement from a Bach Suite.

Paris had been liberated and you were sitting in St Clement Dane's School playing the Minuet from the Boccherini C Major Quintet while girls in coloured bands played netball on the wired-in cage roof of the building opposite you, and roared in gangs arm-in-arm in the street below singing: 'For the Boys will soon be Home'.

You tried to make every note, every movement of wrist and bow and fingers converge into a single blossoming, as though you had been squeezed, expelled, extruded from the hard dead dry leaves of the war; a joyful explusion from the life you were living then.

Once you went with a youth orchestra to play at the Cripplegate Institute in the City. You climbed out of the tube station at Aldersgate. A red Royal Mail van on rubber wheels went silently by, pulled by four horses. You stared round you. The streets for miles around were nothing but low brick walls about a foot high filled with herb robert. Round you, you could see nothing but a waste of dusty buddleia and herb robert. You played that night as though it were the only relevant response to the waste round you, the cello reaching up to take the theme from the viola and carry it up triumphantly, up and away from the desolation all round.

'What terrible days those were' your mother said once, a few years ago, when you had gone to visit her where she still lived in Maisky Street. And you remembered the time when she had promised on her day off to go to a lunchtime concert and had gone swimming instead and when she came in and you asked her how she had enjoyed the Brahms, you had seen her wet hair and found a warm seed packet in her pocket with the milkman's money inside and the purple ticket for 'One Ladies' Swim'. You kissed her when you remembered it.

'What terrible days those were' she repeated. 'I should never have let you come back to London. We should have stayed in Sussex where we were well-off and safe. But I did so much want you to get on.' You were much easier with her now than when you had been a boy, but you said nothing. 'We should have stayed in the country' she repeated. You still said nothing. 'What a war!' she had sighed.

You had celebrated Victory in Europe Day by dancing in Maisky Street, with bunting looped from house to house and big notices at every window: 'Bring our Boys Back Home.'

Six million Jews and twenty million Russians. Yours had been an easy war.

You had won a scholarship to study full time at the Academy in 1947.

'Why don't you go down to Sussex and visit Gran and Gramp?' your mother had suggested. 'They are always asking after you and asking us to go down. Only I never liked to be unpatriotic, what with the war and the trains being so bad.'

So you set off for Sussex. You went to spend the summer with your grandparents. You felt no need to go near Happenden or Offenden, Bligh Woods or Pound Common. They only took you away from where you wanted to be.

CHAPTER VII

Your grandparents lived in a First World War gun emplacement on the cliffs some miles from the Sussex village where
you had lived. A row of them had been built along the
cliffs and since their abandonment in 1918, caravans had
sprung up all along the coast round them.

Your grandparents' emplacement was a concrete circle
with a gun-ramp down the middle which they had turned
into a bed for you. The concrete foundations had been
built up with corrugated-iron sides and roof with windows
let into them level with the cliffs at the back which gave
you a good view out to Beachy Head. Round the outside
of the concrete and corrugated-iron emplacement they had
tried to train wistaria and Virginia creeper but the air was
too salty and the winter winds had long ago pushed them
back into a tangle of undergrowth surrounding 'Sea View'
as the emplacement was called.

Your grandparents came to Eastbourne to meet you.
You hadn't seen them since the day you went to tea with
John Rutt above the undertaker's shop. They didn't recog-
nise you at the station, but you remembered them at once,
Gran walking with a stick because of her arthritis and Gramp
standing a little way ahead of her guiding the train in and
telling it where to stop.

They found an inexhaustible source of amusement in
each other. Your grandfather worked in a cheese factory
and when he got in at six you would have evening tea. At
first you tried to help them wash the dishes afterwards,
but Gramp shook his head:

'Our standards of hygiene are higher maybe than yours. And in any case, we have many a merry quip while we're washing up.'

And they did too. You could hear their laughter as you sat in front of Rosa, the big open stove in the ammunition magazine that they had turned into their parlour. They would roar with laughter at Gran's arthritis which made her knees suddenly crumble under her and she would collapse laughing on the concrete kitchen floor. And she would tease Gramp on his passion for hygiene. You had had a bath and as they were washing up a huge douche of dirty bathwater would pour down into the washing-up basin from the bath perched on a ledge above the kitchen wall.

'Now what made it do that?' Gran would ask.

'That was simply the third law of Inertia' Gramp would reply. 'Everything that rises must fall.'

'Oh I don't believe it.'

'Then just fall in with the laws of science' Gramp would reply as she wiped dirty bathwater off her face and hands. 'Gravity. There is no way of overcoming that.'

'Well, I wish gravity didn't always pick on me,' she would protest.

'Learn to fall in with the laws of nature.'

'All the same, I wish there were some way of preventing the bathwater from doing that so often. And why does it always pick on me? Why doesn't it gush up the lavatory when you are sitting up there smoking and having a nice peaceful old-fashioned crap?'

'Sexual selection and prejudice I expect.'

'What I want to know is why like causes don't have like effects' she would continue her protests as she tried to iron your shirts with the hot flat irons that stood beside Rosa. 'One day I put the iron on and there are four lovely flat shiny shirts. But the next time I do exactly the same thing and bang! There is a great scorch mark over the sleeve. And the same with cooking. I follow the recipe carefully and the blackberry crumble turns out delicious with a shiny brown top. But the next time I try to make it there are nothing but fluffy blobs of flour in a juice that makes the roof of your mouth feel dry like after eating rhubarb or spinach.'

'Oh the laws of cause and effect will never let you down. The trouble with you is that the first time you make a dish it tastes good, so the second time you put in twice the amount, thinking to make the pudding even better.'

'No. It's not that. It's just that the material world won't obey me. I follow the pattern for a dress and what happens? I look like a retarded unmarried mother in something the Women's Voluntary Service has just handed out.'

'Like causes have like effects, and would you mind passing this knife back into the soapy water again and applying some friction to remove all the food fragments that have lodged there.'

'I'll give you food fragments' she would splash a dish-mop full of water into his face. 'How did the food fragments get there in the first place I'd like to know.'

'If I weren't such a poor trencherman . . .'

'You a poor trencherman! What have you just eaten? Kidney and liver and bread and potatoes and three cups of tea!'

'All the same, my constitution is a delicate one. Wind.' He burped. 'Wind.' He farted. 'Why can't we all go back to the simple life and eat bread? Meat is just a relish. What is more wholesome than brown bread with a nice piece of raw spinach leaf placed on top. Full of vitamins. That is all the human frame required. Or a mess of potage.'

'I'd like to see your face if I gave you a mess of potage for your supper. And what about Will? He can't live on a mess of potage.'

'That was what God meant us to live on.'

'Now why did it do that?' Gran would cry as a fork flew out of her hand and landed on a saucer and smashed it.

'That was the second law of attraction and repulsion. A mess of potage is all that the human frame requires at the end of the day.'

So Gran would buy beans and lentils and for three days you would eat nothing but lentil roast and pea soup. Then on the fourth day Gramp would clear his throat and push away his plate and announce:

'I've come to a momentous conclusion. The fish of the sea were made for man's use. Especially fish with black skin. Coley. What is more nutritious than a small portion of coley, and the best part of that coley is the black skin.'

Or Gran would climb into the bath when it was her turn to stoke Rosa up and heat the water. She would finish her bath and then find that her arthritis prevented her from getting out.

'Oh my knees!' she would shout. 'Someone come and help me.' So you would both rush into the kitchen and climb the packing cases that led up to the ledge where the bath stood and both haul on her arms while she collapsed with pain and laughter. 'You'll have to go and call the nieghbours or I shall stay here for ever.'

'System' cried Gramp. 'System in all things.' He stood there and thought. 'Suppose I buy a kind of lilo that you lay on as you washed. Then when you had finished your bath and wanted to get out, all we would have to do would be to inflate the lilo under you, and you would rise gracefully like the Birth of Venus to the rim of the bath while soft music played from down below. "First Floor Ladies' Underwear" and when the lilo reached the top, off you would step and there is Prince Florestan waiting to greet you.' He held out his arms for her, but she was still helpless in the water.

'I'll give you Prince Florestan.'

'It's simply the first law of Hydraulics. But what could be more appropriate than if a simple innocent child got into the bathwater behind you and gave you a gentle lift?' So you would take off your shoes and roll up your trousers and get into the bath and take Gran under the armpits and together you would haul her out.

'Don't you ever get arthritis' she would warn you as you sat round Rosa sipping mulled cider that Gramp always prepared on the night that Gran had her bath.

On Saturdays you would all cycle into Eastbourne. 'Very good for the arthritis' Gramp would say as he and Gran climbed on to the tandem with a small motor attached to the back wheel and you set off, you racing behind on a child's

92

bicycle they had borrowed from some neighbours. You out of breath but trying to keep up with them.

'What is ailing the wee childer?' Gramp would peer back to see where you were. 'Not enough exercise in London. Take a deep breath. Country air.' Then he would set the motor of the tandem going again and you would press on.

Your first stop was at Woods' Herbal Chemist where Gramp would stand fumbling, his money in his hands, meditatively trying to decide whether to take a packet of Smith's Home-brewed French red wine, or a packet of Woods' own best British Bitter.

Then you would go into Woolworth's and buy a record of Gracie Fields singing The Lord's Prayer or some new gadget for unblocking drains, or a Jacko for home-decoration. Then you would buy a pound of fish with black skin.

Once on your way home you passed a field of cowslips.

'Where the cowslips there slip I' Gramp sang as he dismounted. 'What could be nicer than a glass of gracious cowslip wine for gracious living on a cold winter evening?'

'But the field is full of cows,' you objected.

'Man must not yield to God's humblest creation.' He would urge you forward to pick cowslips. Nevertheless you saw a stone in his hand as one of the bullocks approached. He looked at the basket half-full of cowslips and said 'Hmmm. Perhaps it would be violating God's gift to man if we took any more.'

Once on your weekly trip to Eastbourne your grandfather decided that he needed a new suit. You all went into the Forty Shilling Tailor with his clothing coupons. He looked at three suits and pulled out one:

'I'll take this one.'

'But aren't you going to try it on?'

He shook his head: 'No need. I have the normal physique of the Nordic type. The evolutionary type. The type meant to advance civilisation.'

So you left the shop with the bundle; the legs swinging off Gramp's arm and the sleeves off Gran's. There was no paper for wrapping them in those days.

The weather grew hot and you spent your days on the

beach swimming and sunbathing and wandering over the cliffs. When August Bank Holiday came Gran asked: 'Where shall we go this year?'

Gramp shook his head. 'The war isn't over yet. Let's be patriotic. Holidays at home.' So you took sandwiches up to the cliffs and when you got there you looked back at the huddle of caravans and the row of gun-emplacements that you had come from, six miles away.

'What funny things legs are' you said. 'You just put one a few inches in front of the other and give a little push and here we are all the way up here.'

'Legs were invented before wheels' Gramp said munching a spinach sandwich.

'You'd think it would be the other way round' Gran objected. 'You'd think it would be more convenient if men had wheels on their feet to begin with. And just imagine a car or a bus powered by eight or ten legs. It makes me feel sea-sick just to think of all that jerking.'

'All is for the best' said Gramp.

Next day he took you out in the canoe he kept hidden in the blackberry bushes at the bottom of the cliffs. You started to make the journey to Beachy Head but the *Queen Elizabeth* got in your way. Gramp waved her off:

'Ahoy!' he called, 'steam must give way to sail and sail to paddle.' All the same you turned round. That evening he fumbled about in the cupboard and pulled out a piano accordion. 'I could never master the difference between the black notes and the white.' He gave it to you. 'And my fingers could never get round all those notes fast enough. So have it, boy.' He drew the handles apart and a moaning sound came out:

> 'Have you heard that long haired gent?
> Paderewski! What the deuski!' (he sang).
> 'He can play the grand pianer,
> Rusticaner,
> Have a banana . . .
> Up and down those keys he goes.
> Mind your eyebrows, mind your nose.

And they all sit tight in the first ten rows
When Paderewski plays ... Who knows? We
might one day hear you playing this to great gatherings at the
Albert Hall.' He gave it to you. You wondered what your life
would be like now if you had come down here to live for the
duration as your mother had tentatively suggested.

August the sixth and Gramp came home from the caravan
shop with the evening newspaper. Hiroshima. Nagasaki. The
atom bomb. The Japanese had capitulated.

'All is for the best' Gramp read out the news. 'Man must
fall in line with the laws of nature.' He and Gran went down
to the pub to celebrate the end of the war and stayed there
till twelve and came home drunk and arm-in-arm singing
'Happy Days are Here Again'. But this time you didn't feel
like celebrating. The Allies had become one with the forces
they had fought against. You suddenly wanted to return to
London. You needed your cello. You went back home.

In September 1947 you took up your Scholarship at the
Royal Academy. You spent three years there studying all
Bach's Cello Suites, the Brahms No. 2, the Edmund Rubbra
G minor Sonata and all Beethoven's.

'You are still not bringing it to a beautiful *pianissimo* end.
Your *pianissimo* is dry and thin. And remember at bar sixteen you are only echoing the piano. You are playing as
though it were your solo. You must listen to the piano and
reply to it. And let that lovely Cantabile sing. And rise to a
climax on the D. No. Let the weight of your wrist and shoulder hold the bow on those minims. And be nicer to that bar
after the *sforzando*. You are banging it out like a gun going
off. And look towards the piano which is just going to take
up the theme. Pick it up lightly, let it fly up. Don't push it
there. And be more generous to that pause. Give it a lovely
shape. Hear it with your inner ear first.'

You were the cellist in an Academy quartet. You studied
all Schubert's Quartets and some of Mozart's.

'. . . You're not playing as though you meant it. Don't let
that B hang there like washing on a line, viola. And cello, be
nicer to that answering phrase. Respond more sensitively.
Make it a delicate reply. And second violin, not such a deep

vibrato. You are only accompanying here . . .'

Then you first encountered the passion and tragic lyricism and violence of Bela Bartók.

'. . . A rising violence here. No, you're just producing a nasty grating sound in those agitated demi-semi-quavers. Gravity. Think of gravity. The second crescendo has a rising acerbity but you are just turning it into feeding time at the zoo. And how are you going to connect those triplets with that lovely D minor phrase just before? Let your bow sink right inside your string and bring out the inside of that *forte*. No. No. You are playing from your nerves and muscles. And wait. Attend. This is a very melancholic ending but you are just turning it into a military review. Violins, bring out the pathos of that last inverted theme. You are just being rough instead of fevered.'

You joined the Academy first orchestra and studied the symphonies of Beethoven and Brahms. In your third year you studied Tchaikovsky's Rococo Variations and the Dvořák Concerto, and played them at Academy concerts. Then you studied the Saint-Saëns Concerto and won a scholarship to study in France for a year under Charles Hivère.

CHAPTER VIII

'Elle est prise, cette place, ma Soeur,' a woman with a child on the train told a nun with a cardboard suitcase strapped with dry leather bands as you settled your cello above you in the rack. The first thing you had wanted to do when you arrived in Paris was to go and see M. Hivère. But when you telephoned, a child's voice answered:

'Il est souffrant. C'est une crise de foie.' Your French was what you had learned at the South-East London Emergency School, sitting in the school cloakrooms during a raid and singing *'Savez-vous planter les choux?'*

'Il a une crise de foie.' You imagined the French nation from politicians to school-children periodically prostrated by religious crises. 'Ring again next week' you gathered the child was telling you.

You settled yourself in your train compartment. The scholarship paid your tuition fees with Hivère. But it was not enough to live on so you had got yourself a job as an 'assistant anglais' teaching English conversation in a *Cours Complémentaire* for girls about eighty kilometres from Paris.

You sat there in the train having your first lesson in French as you slid out of Paris.

'Un âne. Deux nânes,' the little girl opposite you chanted to her mother staring absently at a donkey in the picture book in front of her.

'Ah non, ma petite. Un âne. Deux ânes.'

'Un sâne. Deux sânes.'

'Ah non, ma petite. Deux ânes. Cinq ânes.'

'Sept' pause *'ânes'* the child said at last smiling and

97

dangling her legs. Her mother kissed her: *'Voilà, ma petite.'*

You pictured your new address at Les Aubraies as you rode through the flat intensively cultivated countryside. 16 Rue de la Câle. You saw a tall grey house, a big stucco house with shutters and balconies and people sitting at the windows or in the cafés beneath in the street where children with long baguettes came out of the bakeries and women walked home from the market with live chickens under their arms.

But Les Aubraies was a modern town, apart from its medieval church, totally rebuilt after the Allied bombings of 1944. You took a taxi from the station. Rue de la Câle was a row of yellow and orange brick villas on the outskirts of the town surrounded by *terrains à vendre*, empty waste plots. The houses were built in the style of the Belgian seaside resorts of the thirties with pink and green gravel covering the front gardens and fancy iron-work gates. Your room had a big double bed, a huge heavy sideboard with a mirror over it, mottled lino and a single chair. Overhead an enormous chandelier hung, a black tin replica of La Sainte Chapelle. In the corner was a cold water tap that dripped into a chipped enamel basin.

'Où est la toilette?' you asked Madame Blin, your landlady.

'Le vataire? C'est à côté.'

'Et le bain?'

'C'est mon bain privé.' She left you with your keys. A thin partition separated your room from the one next door. You could hear a girl and her boy-friend whispering and making the bed rattle. You got out your cello and started to practise. You felt empty. You hadn't practised for several days. You started on some Romberg studies.

'Ah mon dieu! Ces anglais mélomanes,' the girl next door groaned. Then there was a thumping on the partition. You replied by playing the haunting little tune from the Saint-Saëns Concerto. She groaned. They went out.

You walked across the town and crossed over the river and climbed the hill to the top where the *Cours Complémentaire* stood. It was also the local maternity hospital and you could hear the cries of babies from the upper rooms of the school.

You could smell disinfectant and chloroform and newly-cemented tiles. You found the school office:

'*L'emploi du temps n'est pas encore préparé,*' the *surveillante*, a dark, pale-faced girl of about eighteen who introduced herself as Marie-France told you. '*On mange à six heures et demi.*'

You wandered home through the town, through the Botanical Gardens and the Municipal Gardens, across the river where rows of wooden boats stood with women leaning over the sides plunging linen into the river water. You got back to your room. You unpacked. At six-thirty you went back to the school. You crossed the pebbled playground and went into the office. Marie-France took you down to the refectory and introduced you to the kitchen staff as '*le meester anglais*'. You sat down alone in the long empty basement dining room with a mosaic floor and rows and rows of board tables and benches, and bottles of beer for the pupils ranged along the tables.

La dame de la cuisine brought you in a faded tureen of thin parsley soup and thumbs of bread. Then came a bowl of lentils dressed in herbs and oil. Then a long eel in white sauce, then roast turkey and noodles, and a salad of stiff frizzy lettuce that tasted bitter. The meal ended with a large blob of jam in the middle of a large white plate, a bowl of yoghourt, a pear, and finally a slice of Brie with running sides. You ate alone; outside the refectory your future pupils were chattering outside the door waiting for you to finish.

'*Qu'est-ce qu'on mange, meester?*' they asked as you came out. '*Quand commencent nos cours d'anglais?*'

'*Et des correspondantes, meester.*' '*Des correspondantes anglaises.*'

For the next month you took delicious meals up at the school and presented yourself daily at the school office where the *surveillante* would tell you that the time-table had still not been completed. You would ring Paris and try to speak to M. Hivère. But always the same incomprehensible reply came. He was '*souffrant*'. '*Il a une crise de nerfs*' or he was on holiday.

You would cross the *préau* to get to the school. The cry of babies came. The smell of chloroform. The pupils would be standing round in knots tapping balls against a wall or singing French songs or learning English verbs. Once you asked Marie-France if you could have a bath at the school.

'*C'est notre bain privé,*' she shook her head. There was one small lavatory for the whole school, a dark windowless cupboard at the end of the long dormitory where the pupils slept during the week.

They came from miles around and stayed at the school till Saturday evening. When they weren't in class, they were *en étude*. On Saturday evenings their fathers came with horses and traps, small *cultivateurs* from the flat countryside of peasant farms round the town.

You admired their politeness, raising their caps to you as they came in to the office to collect their daughters and sign them off for the week-end. Sometimes they couldn't read or write and their daughters would do it for them and then they would shake hands all round: '*Au revoir mesdames, monsieur. A lundi.*'

The pupils brought nothing to school each week except their nightclothes in a paper bag. Boarding-school life was simple. There were no wardrobes, or suitcases or lockers by the beds. At first you were surprised by the long bare dormitory, the brown hospital blankets, the little rolled hard sausage pillows a foot away from the folded-over edge of the unbleached sheets. You thought of Paddington and Victoria stations and girls and boys going back to school with school uniform, indoor shoes, outdoor shoes, games shoes, trunks, first night cases, crests on the blazers, emblems on their hats, hockey sticks, morning prayers, and ends of term:

'Three cheers for our Head! . . . Three cheers for our Prefects! . . . Three cheers for our School! . . .' And then there would be 'Jerusalem' and 'God Save Our King' you would imagine.

You loved the economy of this French school life. They didn't try to make school into anything but an intellectual disciplining. They didn't try to form character or create Christians or impart patriotism or make the school one large happy family. Everything was hard and austere and you would watch the pupils in the *préau* at five when classes ended, excitedly eating their crusts of dry bread and jam before the bell went for *étude*. They seemed waiting excitedly for adulthood.

There was still no word from the school about your teaching hours and no word from Hivère in Paris. You practised. You prepared Shostakovitch's Sonata, Opus 40, for him, and the Schumann Concerto. When you got tired of the rude comments from the room on the other side of the partition you strolled down to the river to watch the barges at the lock, or went to the cinema.

'Est-il complet?' you asked once when you were refused admission.

The girl at the guichet looked at you puzzled for a moment, then she nodded: *'Nous avons beaucoup d'adhérents ce soir.'*

You rolled the phrase round and round on your tongue. You compared it delightedly with 'Is it full?' You were beginning to love the French tongue, and the formality of the way the French took their pleasure. Marie-France would take a night off to *faire un tour* of the town, or she would go to a patisserie with a friend and eat a *mille feuilles* and drink a glass of water and talk, standing in the little shop talking and laughing till she was obliged to return to the office at ten.

In November your classes at last started. You faced forty pupils, the older ones mending their nylons discreetly under the desks.

'Good morning, meester,' they would greet you. But your French was too poor to control them. Marie-France would come and shout at them to line up in the *préau*:

'Rangez-vous, les élèves.' Or she would stand in the doorway of the classroom when the noise from your room was too great: *'Taisez-vous, les élèves.'* And for a moment there was quiet.

The set text for the twelve-year-olds was Lord Baden Powell's *Scouting for Boys*. At first you tried to get them interested in cold swims and canoeing and tracking. Then you wrote to the British Council in Paris for help with teaching materials. They sent you back pictures of Princess Elizabeth in a Girl Guide uniform talking to a lot of poorly-clad East End children.

'Les pauvres,' the pupils would sigh, attending to their long white socks and pleated skirts and navy-blue overalls. You tried to teach them English but it offended your aesthetic sense that the pupils, off whose tongues the French language would roll like oil pouring smoothly out, should twist up their mouths and faces as though they were about to sneeze and croak out: 'Cake . . . Book . . . Cock . . .' and that the smoothness of their olive faces should be deformed by the harshness of 'Put . . . Box . . . Bucket . . . Bacon.' They would giggle as they pronounced the barbarous words:

'Meester, quand aura-t-on des correspondantes anglaises?'

One twelve-year-old had a pen-friend in Catford. 'What does "smooching" mean?' she asked you one day. 'My pen-pal' ('Pen-pal' the pupils would giggle and chant), 'my pen-pal says she likes smooching.'

'Smooching' the rest of the class would chant, distorting their faces.

You solved the problem of what to teach them by playing the piano and teaching them English songs. 'Speed Bonnie Boat' and 'Early One Morning' or if you were desperate because you still had half an hour to kill before the bell went for the end of classes, you would start them off singing 'Three Blind Mice' or 'London's Burning' or 'White Sands and Grey Sands' in rounds of four parts that kept them going till the end of the afternoon.

Autumn leaves swooped and banged down suddenly on to the playground like hawks over their prey. At *La Toussaint*, All Souls' Day holidays, you went to Normandy and walked on the bare beaches and ate *fruits de la mer* in cafés on the sea-front, and were amused by the *Stations Balnéaires* (beaches), the *Instituts Thalassiques* (swimming-pools), the *Cours d'Education Physique* (tennis courts) or the *Instituts de Beauté* (hairdressers). You stayed in Normandy wandering from resort to resort and climbing the cliffs for the whole of the five days' holiday. Your cello had temporarily abandoned you, as though the temperature of a greenhouse had dramatically dropped in the night and when you went there the flowers had all died.

'*Rangez-vous, les élèves,*' Marie-France would cry as the bell went in the *préau* and the evening's studies were to begin. You would wander off down to the river, have a bath in the Municipal Baths, and stand watching *les lavandières* in their big wooden laundry boats moored to the banks, talking, shouting, laughing as they plunged the dirty clothes into the river, shouting and beating them with pumice stone and laughing when they had to break the ice in winter.

On the train coming to Les Aubraies you had met a woman who spoke English and she had given you the address of the Club de la Jeunesse. 'You won't find yourself too lonely.' She had written the address down for you and in this lull in your relationship with your cello you had gone there and met a girl called Giselle who spoke good English. She had a mass of frizzy red hair and wore wire-spectacles and '*pantalons existentialistes*'.

You had gone to the pictures together. It was a film about the life of Van Gogh.

'*Nous avons beaucoup d'adhérents*' . . . 'We are full up.' You had mulled over the characteristics of the two phrases. You admired the French for their precision, their clearly delineated rules of politeness and their carefully plotted contours of work and pleasure. You tried to express this to Giselle. She only scoffed:

'*Nous avons beaucoup d'adhérents* . . . Bourgeois pomposity! That's all.'

Christmas came and you wanted to go home and visit your mother but you still had not heard from Charles Hivère. So you spent Christmas with Giselle. She had lit a fire of wood in the black iron stove in the room which she rented from an old lady, and invited two girls in and you ate a tangerine each and danced to the music of the gramophone. Then at ten the old lady came in and you shook hands and drank a glass of wine each and a *gâteau sec* and shook hands again and went home. That was your Christmas day and you were happy as you wandered home along the riverside *Quai* under the stars. 'How clever I am,' you thought, 'to have found work and a livelihood in this little French town that no one has ever heard of.' But you still had not heard from Hivère.

It was Epiphany and the *Fête des Rois* when you got back to the school. The domestics had made a large circular cake shaped like a crown and filled it with nuts and spice and angelica. In it they had put a one franc piece and the pupil who got it was King for the day and wore a paper crown and led a long chain of pupils chanting round and round the school. There were no lessons that afternoon. You still sometimes rang Hivère in Paris but you rarely understood the reply. You practised Romberg studies. You prepared the Schumann Cello Concerto.

Spring came and Giselle invited you home one week-end to her family at St Pol les Bresses. You travelled on the bus with your bikes put on top and got them off at Hièges and cycled the last five miles to the village and ate chicken stuffed with walnuts and apricots. Giselle's mother showed you how to hold your left wrist against the table as you ate and Giselle picked at her salad and snorted at her mother for trying to make you believe that there was a French culture and an English one rather than a single Capitalist one that overrode all the niceties of the table. And you and Giselle had left her parents to take their Sunday afternoon walk up to the cemetery and had gone down to the harbour and watched the small wooden boats chugging out for the night, then you walked as far as La Rosée and sat in a café all afternoon over one cup of coffee.

'I've never seen how English you are' Giselle said 'until I see you beside my family.'

Spring came and you cycled to Dombray and Nièze, to Aulnay and La Follentin. The names grew more and more beautiful to you until you felt you must make love to Giselle simply because you loved France so much.

You lay among the gorse bushes. You slid your hand across her belly and stretched it from one pelvic bone to the other. The roof of your mouth tingled and shook. You slid your hands into the crease between her buttocks and eased her legs apart. She steered you over her breasts and her clitoris, but then you were fiddling with a French letter and she was crying: 'Come on. Come quickly!' And then when you penetrated her she cried: 'Too late. *Les anglais sont mous et amorphes.*' You had to look the words up.

Hivère wrote in March. You climbed excitedly into the high Paris train with your cello. You took a taxi to his house at Passy. You waited half an hour in his salon then he came in. He had the largest tallest broadest forehead you had ever seen, with a bristle of red hair round its edges. You played him the first movement of the Schumann. He waited till the end.

'Why do you hug it so close to you? Ze English constipation. You must give zat first entry to the world, not keep it so close to yourself. Da-dee! You have no sense of contour or outline. You play as though you were a sheep in a field, blank and surprised and startled to find himself the only sheep in the field.' You spent the whole lesson on the cello's first entry: '*Mou et amorphe*' Hivère cried.

'Do you really think I am *"mou"* and *"amorphe"*?' you asked Giselle when you got back.

You went back to Hivère with the second movement. He had cut himself shaving that morning and did not appear. You went back once more in June. He leaned back in his seat:

'You are using too much bow. And your *pianissimos* are dead and lifeless. Sin and scratchy and you do not let zem breaze or sing. And your rests and pauses have no shape, no beginning and end.' He wiped his nose and smiled: 'I have ze feeling zat you are very very aingry vis me.'

'I've hardly had time to be. On what grounds?'

'Oh, just a hunch.' He squeezed his big knuckles together till they shone white. 'Why all zis ainger? A beautiful tone vill only come from a humble and joyful heart. But your strings vibrate viz your ainger. I can feel it coming from your shoulder and your heart, zis buzz.'

'But what makes you think I'm so angry?'

'Just a hunch' he shrugged. He talked a bit about tone colour. 'But why all zis competition? All zis competitiveness?'

'Competitive? Give me an example . . .'

'Oh just a hunch. Why are you so anxious to become a famous artist? Why do you not settle down in Finchley or Mill Hill' he chuckled at the thought of these places, 'and

105

teach little English girls who love always to have somesing between zeir legs . . . Horses . . . A cello . . . And get yourself a lovely cello.'

You never saw him again. He was off to America on a recital tour. You went back to the railway station in a fever. You could hardly wait for the train to pull out. You went straight back to Rue de la Câle without stopping for dinner at the school. Giselle came but you only smiled and pecked at her forehead and she went and you undid your cello and played Bach and Brahms and Boccherini and the Schumann as though a great flood of water at the top of a dam were bursting at you from the outside, and you were just a piece of machinery for refining it into sound. You did not stop playing till the girl from next door came in at two:

'Est-ce qu'elle est presque finie, cette histoire lamentable?'

You went to Paris next day and bought yourself a new cello. It wasn't an old one. It had been made by Louis Bertrand in 1877, but it had a sweet tone. On its C string it was sad and plangent like a viola da gamba and near to weeping, but in its upper register it raised its voice as if in some grave discontent with matter.

You thought of your past as you sat in the little churchyard gardens beside your block of flats. You thought of how your cello had converted your childhood's valley of shadows into a passion for life; of how you had transcended the presence of death. But now your mouth felt dry and your thoughts flew back to Happenden and Offenden and the tide rising in the river to take you.

CHAPTER IX

You walked down Theobald's Road to the Gordon Hall where you rehearsed. The dazzling green volcanoes of the trees along the sides of the road comforted you. Perhaps the green would lift you up and take you if you turned your back on hope and waited in darkness.

You unlocked the doors of the hall and went in and started to unpick the Wersby quartet before the others arrived. It was rough and harsh and turbulent, but suddenly at its most sore and disjointed it burst out into its faraway A major tune, beginning as a chorale on muted strings, a haunting tune like a May morning hymn that suddenly goes wrong and turns itself inside out into a wild pagan tune of endless surging prehistory.

The quartet arrived and you began to play. The viola came in on a long high sustained A, the cello crept up to it in staccato jerks. The first violin waited to seize the cello's crescendo and turn it into silence. A shaped silence, a pause that gave a sudden resonance to the dotted minims that ended it.

For a moment you thought your drought had gone as you played this quartet you had never played before with its rough anger, its sudden silences encapsuled in the sword play of the two violins. But the struggle and the resistance were suddenly forgotten, or rather emptied out, discarded, unresolved, and the May morning tune came at first serene and joyful but then the cello took it up and turned it inside out into a terrible message: 'Then die, Prince, die.'

Nancy had the tune and she passed it over to you and you received it joyfully. You smiled at Nancy and blessed her.

107

But as you received the message it became a terrible one 'Then die, Prince, die!' and you lost it. The process of playing music had become more physically and mentally agonising than unsuccessful love-making.

George put down his bow and wiped his eyes:

'Is that a B flat or a B natural? I suggest that one of us goes round to Wersby's flat and tries to find the original manuscript. This is so badly photostated. Wersby's agent says he hasn't got it. The only place it can be is in his flat. Will, you used to know Wersby, didn't you? Would it be possible for you to go round there before we rehearse tomorrow and see if you can find the original score?' You nodded. 'Then at least we shall know we are playing what the composer intended.' You nodded again.

'I must love you and leave you' Nancy muttered. 'I must get Basket back from the vet before four.'

You packed your cello and went out into the Theobald's Road. A man in a T-shirt with 'Soft Ranch' written across the chest was talking:

'A suitcase full of Sunday dinner. Even the Yorkshire pudding was there.'

'And he wakes me at two and then goes right out.'

'Yes, you should do, but who knows?'

You went into the churchyard gardens and sat down. A middle-aged woman and her mother sat at the next bench eating a cheese sandwich each:

'Too cheesy for me.' The food bulged from their mouths.

'Here, put some in mine.' The cheese rose and passed from one bread roll to the other. The women ate. Then the daughter put two cigarettes in her mouth and flicked on a lighter and lit them both. A blue flower, a blue lily flowed from the end of the lighter, swayed and disappeared. She handed a cigarette over to her mother:

'Yes, she was a dresser up at the Palladium . . . You had to have nimble fingers then when the quick-fire variety was on . . .'

'If the bed doesn't go through again . . .'

'And Wednesday was all right . . .'

'But it come out square with two march valves . . .'

'And sugar on top. Right the way through you get them . . .'
('Oh send my roots rain.')

Once the dry world of voices and things was the *raison d'être* of your music. But now it only led you away into the overwhelming green of oblivion. 'Then die, Prince, die!'

You went towards Cafford Square where Wersby lived. You didn't even bother to go home and leave your cello. Thelma would be in. Thelma would be in.

You knew Cafford Square where John Wersby had lived. You had no need to look it up on the London Street Map. You had climbed the hill between Finsbury and Islington nearly every day for two years when you lived with him.

You could see the spires of St Pancras from the top of the hill and the tower-blocks of Hampstead and Kentish Town. Then you turned right between the terracotta fortress tenements — Hogben Buildings and Denman House with tin baths and birdcages and bicycles tied to the railings on the open staircases and you knew exactly how Cafford Square would rear up with its triangular pediments behind them as the street opened out into the square. Sudden peace would come like the sound of a heavy motorbike being gradually extinguished as it flies on into the night.

You came upon the four white terraces quietly. There was the green square in the middle where old men sat and children rollerskated, arranged their dolls along the seats or played hopscotch on the paths. There was the huge flowering chestnut in the corner thrusting its scarlet breasts out at you in May. Cafford Square stood like the rim of a palace seen light through the dark.

It had been shabbier then than now. The white plaster facades had been peeling and leprous then. The white pilasters beside its front doors had run up to fanlight windows that had most of them been broken and stuffed with old newspapers or boarded up with cardboard. But now two sides of the square had been replastered and repainted. Georgian windows shone green at you in the afternoon light as you crossed the square.

Some of the basements in the redecorated side, you saw, had now been turned into gleaming steel kitchens with double sink units, or into children's nurseries with rocking horses and playpens and indoor swings in the windows. The fine lines of the front-door fanlights had been painted white and the wrought-iron balconies a glowing black.

On the other side though, the terraces were still grey and peeling, with dirty net curtains or newspaper or old table-cloths dragged straight across the windows and damp basements smelling of tomcats where thin old faces lurked at windows and doors fearfully for the landlord. There were faded rain-washed grit-smeared cards by the front-door bells listing eight or ten tenants. In one house you remembered that a picture of the Sacred Heart pierced with a sword stopped up the broken fanlight. It was still there. Another you remembered still had a statue of the Virgin with a vacant smile that lit up at night.

Wersby's flat was in the unreconstructed part of the square. He had been a controlled tenant, you seemed to remember.

You would come home from rehearsal or performance – you were playing in the B.B.C. Symphony Orchestra then – and find him in his living room with its plasma red walls, bare floor, trestle table and camp chair working at his song-cycle or his Septet. Or he had just finished *The Good Soldier Schweik* – he had been commissioned to write it for a film – and had bought a bottle of wine to celebrate its completion. He was a vegetarian and you would bring your own food in and sit there eating while he opened the bottle.

'Delicious lamb chops! How can you be a vegetarian?' you ate. 'When God named the animals to man in the Garden of Eden, he named the lamb as especially delicious.'

'If God had meant ma-ma-man to eat the animals' Wersby had a bad stammer and blurted his words out slow then fast. You watched his unmatching hands as he opened the bottle. The left one bigger than the right one through playing a viola that was too big for him as a child. He had short cropped red hair and a long incompleted white face. His eyes were strong and green and incisive but the crooked nose and the unaligned mouth gave his face a robbed and cheated look, incomplete or badly put together.

'. . . If G-Go-God had meant' he stuttered 'men to eat

animals, he would have tied them on trees like fruit.' You went on eating. Wersby had uncorked the bottle and was pouring out the wine.

'Cheers' you drank. 'Hmmm. Good. I wonder why they always keep the best wine till the end?'

'It was the ma-marriage at Caana that did it. Christ could hardly have produced plonk when he was told they had run out of wine at the wedding. He could hardly have turned water into plonk.'

'John' you had asked him at one of these sober little celebrations when you both drank a couple of glasses of Côte du Rhône or Moselle, and Wersby ate a plate of boiled carrots with cheese grated on top and you ate bread and garlic sausage, 'John, why don't we have a party to celebrate *The Good Soldier Schweik*?'

'Parties don't say anything to me' he replied stiffly. 'Whom were you proposing to invite?'

'A few friends from the orchestra and perhaps Annery.'

Annery was the conductor who had discovered John Wersby as a self-taught young man of twenty-three serving as a bandsman in a Guards Regiment. It was Annery who had arranged for his youthful symphony to be played at a Promenade Concert. But there the orchestra had rubbished him, dragging the rhythm, failing to come in at the right places and turning the work into a rhetorical patriotic march for 'Empire Day' or Armistice Sunday. It was an experience that had made him withdraw from other musicians and never write for an orchestra again. It was this experience that had led him to a new style — he never wrote for more than six or ten instruments now, and had abandoned the key and the diatonic scale. He had told you this when you met him later at a Dartington Hall summer music school where you were playing and where you were both teaching. You had liked him and admired his music and his sincerity and his stoical reserve, and when he had mentioned to you that he had a room he wanted to let you had gone to see it and stayed two years. Your playing at that time was a struggle against the desert and emptiness and unmeaning that you felt all round you and it succeeded then. You were twenty-seven and he

111

was thirty and in him you found an uncompromising companion with similar sympathies.

'Let's give a party.' He pulled down his long thin face. You knew he had never had the art of conversation. He would listen to people talking and said it was often as incomprehensible as an opera in a foreign language, as meaningless as its synopsis and its characters mouthing animatedly at completely meaningless phrases and responding with equal excitement to these unknowns.

It was when you were still living with him two years later in 1958 that you went to your first Campaign for Nuclear Disarmament meeting at Central Hall, Westminster, on February 17, and came back anxious to convert him:

'A million dead and lethal fall-out on another million . . . Who would want to inflict this on any country, Capitalist or Socialist? Better red than dead.'

Wersby was sitting at his trestle table in his bare red-walled living room. He went on working:

'If ma-ma-man is doomed to destroy himself then he will.'

'But it is the artist's function to affirm life not to connive in self-destruction. If the West has this fascination for self-extinction, it is the artist's business to reinstate the human.'

'The insects will survive. They love heat and drought. This grave dissatisfaction with self and life can only be overcome by art. The Bomb would only be a distraction to my music.'

'But it's the first reality to anyone who cares about life rather than just the preservation of the status quo, and the most efficient way of killing the greatest number of civilians. C.N.D. is the first real struggle against desert and drought and a world scorched to shingle. That is what I struggle after when I play. I was brought up in London during the war.'

'So was I.'

'But I haven't really known till now what precisely I am playing for. But now I see it clearly. To have life more abundantly. Life is too serious for "zones of influence" and politicians' games.'

'The issue is all wars.'

'The Bomb is a beginning. Oh I am so happy. This is the start of a great refusal. The greatest issue there can be for an

112

artist. How can an artist whose aim is to heighten consciousness not stand up against the Cold Warriors using civilians as
bargaining power in their own ideological games?'

'The state is the state whether it bans the Bomb or not.'

'So how can the artist not take sides? How can he fail to
stand up and be counted?'

'The artist takes sides when he plays or composes. I'm not
going to waste my time carrying a banner "John Wersby says
No!" Who cares what John Wersby or Jilly Pendleton-Smith
think about the Bomb?'

'That kind of argument is the way people let Totalitarianism in during the thirties.'

There was a pause. Wersby went on writing then rubbing
out then gathering the rubber and paper shavings onto a card
and tipping them into the waste-paper basket. 'My work is
my contribution to peace.' But you were excited by the
comradeship of that meeting with its packed overflow halls
and you wanted to convert all your fellow-men.

'So what about that party?' you asked a few days later
when John had sent off *The Good Soldier Schweik*. 'Why
don't we invite Annery as well? Why don't you try to get to
know him again? And get him interested in your work again?
He might be able to help you.'

'Help me?' Wersby froze. 'Thank you for your solicitous-
ness. But I've got no small talk and that's all parties are. And
I don't like or trust Annery. Nor do I need his helping hand
to "put me on the map" thank you.'

'You drag me down' you said as Thelma had said yesterday.
'You don't give me any feed-back. Here in this flat I live in a
state of sensory privation. Lack of stimulus. It will rob me of
my ability to play if I go on living in this limbo place.' You
put your jacket on.

'Where are you off to?'

'Just going for a drink. Maybe I shall get some comradeship in the "Crown". Maybe some nice person will come over
and talk to me. Or maybe perhaps if I'm lucky a sympathetic
barman will say "Hullo" to me and I shall be able to shout
back "Hullo". That piece of contact would make my day.
"Hullo!"' you shouted. 'How nice to hear a human voice

actually talking to me. I find you so meticulous and lacking in humanity.'

Wersby went back to his work, rubbing out a cluster of dotted quavers and replacing them by one minim.

'Who are our friends then?'You went over and peered into his face. 'We haven't got any. Only my friends and you never let me invite them in.'

'I've never stopped you.'

'No, but when they come you sit in stony silence with a look of total boredom on your face. Then you start to fidget and yawn and they go. Why the hell do you spend your time playing "Melody Date" in the parks and "Our Royal Land" at Brighton Pavilion? You'd do better to sweep the streets for a living.'

'I just want things to go on as they are. My life as it is. I've tried working in a fish-paste factory and all that. But "Melody Date" stimulates my own kind of anti-music.'

'And makes it all the more inhuman. It's like some mite or flea having an orgasm. You have lost contact with ordinary people as well as with other musicians. I find life so boring here. After a day's rehearsing I want some relaxation.'

'You should get yourself a television set' Wersby said coldly. 'Or a cat. Or take up Patience.'

'Why don't you try and get yourself put on the map?'

'My work is not like that.'

'Or why not try to write music that a musician can at least remember even if he doesn't exactly enjoy playing it. Modern music has no fecundity. It has no tendrils. Nothing clings to it. That's why it's so hard to memorise.'

'That's you. Not the music.'

You remembered the words as you crossed Cafford Square more than fifteen years later. Association was what you missed as you grew older. The smell of burning serge would take you back to 1944 and to the character of your own life then during the war. Music that you had first heard in your teens and twenties and early thirties you could never hear again without its bringing back to you the place where you first discovered it, the exact features of the room or hall, the state of the war or the Cold War, what you were doing at the

114

time, what you were studying, whether you were happy or depressed, what your hopes were. You remembered the first time you played an arrangement of Bach's 'Bist Du bei Mir' ... your mother at the piano, the slanting shelf with the child's doll on it, the bite out of the gas-poker in your mother's flat, the siren going. And when you played Alban Berg, you were back again in France teaching and studying under Charles Hivère in his Passy flat. And when you played Ligeti you were brought back to the first great days of C.N.D., the cold wet smell of the marchers, the sun suddenly breaking through and making your clothes steam. And the quotation from Chekhov's *Three Sisters* would come to you: ... 'One day life will be so beautiful . . .' These recalls would come back to you from your youth. But from your forties nothing came. From your recent married life with Thelma nothing was extracted. Smells and sounds from these years evoked nothing. The years without tendrils had concertina'd together. Nothing stamped itself indelibly on your mind as Beethoven's First Cello Sonata brought back the creaking of the steel bunks in the Oval tube station, the siren gone, the searchlights' silver sword-fights over the dark night sky. All your associations went backwards to your youth only. 'And now I often wish the night had borne my breath away.'

'Is there any white paper?' he had called out to you, 'to line the bread bin with. There are breadcrumbs in the bottom and they seem to be going mouldy. Mouldy. Ugh!'

You laughed.

'Mouldy guts.'

'Only a few old breadcrumbs.' But Wersby went on:

'Something stinks in here. The water in that vase is going rotten.' He sniffed round the sink. 'Something going rotten.' He stood in the kitchen separating knives from forks and glasses from saucepans. He picked up some cotton cloth. 'You surely didn't use this to clean your window? You must never do that. It might scratch the window. And the rag smells funny, as though it were rotting too. And the water in the kettle is stale. Do you always empty it first before you fill it up again? You should. Otherwise our flat will stink.'

'Your flat. Not mine.'

115

'But I wanted it to be ours.' He peered into the dustbin then sniffed round the sink again with a tortured expression on his white face. 'I've got it. It's the blades of these scissors. They've got meat fragments stuck on them. That's what's causing the bad smell. And my mouth tastes bitter. It must be that the inside of the casserole is melting off and poisoning us. Yes, the casserole is just melting away' he gave a shudder. 'Lead glaze. That's it. It will cause us both brain damage. I can feel it in my mouth. Where are you off to?'

'Going round to the "Crown" to get drunk.'

'Why? I've located the . . . the . . . the bad smell.'

'Because you remind me of my aunt Phoebe.'

He woke you at four next morning. 'Help me! I've had such a terrible dream. I was in some recording studios and I was smashing their installations. And when I burst each one like a balloon white sticky stuff came out and onto my face and into my mouth.' You fell asleep again. He woke you half an hour later: '. . . and flowers so big that they started to eat me. Then my mother came with a big bunch of them that she had picked off the railway cutting at the end of the garden. "They never lose their blue, do they John?" she was saying. But that blue. That terrible blue . . .' But you were asleep again and you left the flat next day and soon after that met Thelma. You had known her father, and she was the secretary of your local C.N.D. group.

You only met Wersby casually and infrequently after your marriage, and you were never invited to Cafford Square. Once you invited him to Bude Mansion in the Gray's Inn Road but he never turned up.

But he had taught you to accept the given without deforming it, without transforming it into more or less than the composer had intended. And he had taught you to make a certain gesture of poverty before you began to play, an emptying of yourself before every encounter with music; to open yourself to what it should say without preconceptions; to encounter the non-tangible good objectively as it was. A pure encounter which is not mine and cannot be made into mine; an encounter with that which cannot be corrupted, or by a subtle symbiosis be turned into 'this', 'ours' rather than

'The Other'. He had taught you to wait attentively on music as a religious waits on God.

But the obsession was lost now, as though thieves had come in the night and stolen your virtue away, and now you wanted John Wersby back and he was dead.

You stood in Cafford Square on the shabby side. The white pediments opposite you reared up arrogantly. A bus purred sleekly along the Pentonville Road. Its brakes hissed and there was silence except for the birds clappering on the roofs. You rang the bell marked 'Wersby'. Under the name someone had added: 'Mackery, Chatland and Kyd.' The red flowering chestnut in the corner of the square thrust itself out at you as you stood there. The leaves came out at you with a gush like shining green oil spurted from rich lobes of rock in the dark below. You rang the bell again. A window was lifted in the top floor of the house. A black man with an Afro and wire spectacles and a scarlet polo-necked sweater put his head out.

'I've come to see about some music that John Wersby left' you shouted up. 'His agent has asked me to come.' The black man threw a key down. It landed in the basement. You went down the area steps. An old woman with watery eyes peered out from her door:

'Is it me you want, love? Have you brought something for me?'

You unlocked the front door. It was still as stiff as fifteen years ago. You had to put your shoulder against it and push. You climbed the dark stairs. The West Indian stood there waiting for you at the top of the last flight, his face black and flat like a plate, his eyelids huge and jutting. He held them lowered as he watched you.

'My name's Parrish and I used to live here once with Wersby, and I'm trying to find one of the works he wrote before he died. It's rather urgent. Our quartet is supposed to be playing it at a memorial concert next week and we've only got badly photostated copies and we must find the original.'

The black man looked at you through his wire spectacles. He put his finger on the side of his nose as though he were trying to suppress a sneeze. Then he covered his face with his

117

hands. He said nothing.

'Is it all right if I come in?' The black man still said nothing. He gave a yawn and dropped his huge eyelids and covered his mouth with his hands. He was neat and slim and his buttocks were like two small firm tomatoes rising and falling in his white jeans as he moved, gesturing you in.

'We've had enough trouble with the fuzz,' he said at last. 'Jack' he called into the living room, 'there's a chap here who wants to look through the music.' A smell of stewed meat and cooking oil came from the kitchen. He let you in reluctantly. There was Wersby's bust of Bach. Someone had fixed scooter goggles over the eyes. A rusty motor-cycle carburettor leaned against the bust of Webern. The black man still stood there saying nothing. Two black men and one white girl were sitting on the floor playing cards. There were piles of clothes everywhere and stacks of china and books.

'Waiting for the auctioneer' the white girl said. 'He didn't leave a will.' Among the piles of knives and forks was a photograph of yourself. The squatters stopped their game and sat there very still watching you.

'Would you like a cup of coffee?' the girl asked.

'Thanks. Where did he keep his music?' But you knew. The black man pointed at the cupboard. That was the only piece of furniture in the room apart from the trestle table and the one camp chair . . . the cupboard bursting with manuscripts. Wersby's viola stood on top of it. The black man held it like a guitar and plucked its strings; plucked out a little tune: 'Busy Doing Nothing'.

You sat on the floor and opened the cupboard. 'Share your music' the other black man, thin with long skinny arms and legs coming out of his clothes like a child's drawing of a man, turned a transistor on. You started going through the cupboard, laying the papers systematically in piles. Half-completed manuscripts. A song-cycle of five unfinished songs. An opera still wrapped in the brown paper that the agent had sent it back in when he rejected it. It was not until seven o'clock that you found what was clearly the manuscript of your quartet, the last thing that Wersby had apparently written before he died. Over the second movement was scrawled:

118

'A milkman's cheery whistle heard over the clamour of a public execution.'

You wanted to take all the music away and go through it slowly. But you would need a taxi, and you were anxious to get back home and start rehearsing the Benjamin Britten Cello Symphony that you were playing at Sussex University next month. You asked the two black men standing there watching you whether you could come back next week and collect some more of the stuff.

'A court order' they shrugged. 'An eviction order. Next week. The neighbourhood's going up and they don't want black people here.'

'I'm sorry' you said weakly.

'We shouldn't have put our names on the front door' the skinny young man in a silky blue T-shirt with 'Oxford University' written across the chest twirled Wersby's viola bow.

'Goodbye and thanks.' You turned out of Cafford Square and walked down to Rosebery Avenue. Why had he died? — 'A milkman's cheery whistle' — And would you die like that too since you had grown so much like him?

There was a sudden spread of sun and new green leaf as you walked down Rosebery Avenue. The plane trees caught you with their sudden soft green flesh bursting out of hard woody twigs and dry rusty metallic trunks. A fat fringe of green hung over everything as though overnight the earth had been turned inside out and this soft vegetable dance from the underparts of the city had taken over for a month before it drew back into the flat deflation of high summer. The green pushed along the roof guttering and thrust itself out of the sides of chimneys and inflated the cracks in the battlements of the red brick mansions. Perhaps, it was this sudden new green life that Wersby had felt excluded from that had led to his death. Everything breathing and blooming except me. Or suddenly in January snow had fallen, snow falling down and round and up, circling the houses and growing big and swelling and bulging off the roof tops, making high altars of light on Hogben Buildings, dazzling white altars rising from the black roofs of Denman House, as though even snow had its

119

own fat brewing life and only you were excluded from this miraculous growth. Man thirsts and must die, though life is bursting up round him. Was that why he had died?

You sat down on the green square where the buses turned and old men shuffled among the pigeons. 'All For You and the Family Too' a van passed. The cigarette of the woman sitting next to you on the bench burned down till it reached a piece of sticking plaster on her finger. The smell of singeing cloth came up at you. It reminded you of the burning serge smell when the furniture factory got a direct hit during the war, and the charred cloth bookbindings when a flying bomb got the paper factory where your mother worked and you went to the hospital and found her crying in traction while the nurse brushed plaster and glass out of her hair. Wersby had remained totally detached and indifferent to the war, he once told you.

You sat in the square. A thrush lowered itself on to the dry soil and plugged itself into the core of an ebullient worm locked in the powdery grey earth. Then suction. Then struggle. The plug torn out. The worm swinging against its master's maculated breast. The thrush swinging up with the worm. The carrion crow winging off with the duck's egg in its beak. The python distended with the shape of the whole deer inside it. The elderly man bounced off the front of the passing car, his limbs twitching like a fly on its back before he lay still. Or the people of Hanoi climbing into concrete tubes at the roadsides as the B 52's fragmentation bombs came down. It seemed unlikely that Wersby had died because of that.

Or the black youth. You walked along thinking of him in Wersby's flat, his long slender legs in their tight white jeans and his small round buttocks and his hands covering his mouth as though to fend off a blow, and his huge eyelids coming down. You wanted to take his hands away from his face and hold them. You thought of Thelma waiting soberly and invasively at the flat for you. ('We're going to have a nice supper and then we are going to sit down together and share the Budapest Quartet. Then later we'll draw up a list for our party'.) You saw the thrush flying up again with its swinging

120

worm:

> 'And find my long lost boy,
> And lead me to his joy'

you dreamed softly as you walked along seeing another red chestnut tree in flower like the black man's sweater, his red sweater. His wire glasses. His huge shutter eyelids. His hands across his face and his silent waiting presence. You saw him standing there under the chestnut tree beckoning to you, but when you got there to speak to him he had gone:

'Go away, old unhappy man' as they had wanted to cry at Beethoven when he was deaf and attempted to conduct *Fidelio*. Perhaps that was why Wersby had died. The black man had cursed him.

You walked on. The green throbbed out at the thought of him, the green like a fatal cut made in the pavement and you had woken to find this unstemmable flooding bleeding. May always filled you with a frisson of pleasure at its sudden gush, the sap rising in the twigs and pumping them up into a naked vegetable cataclysm. But now it gave you a shiver of anxiety. The green haemorrhage would flood your brain unstemmably and take you even further away from where you wanted to be. Perhaps that was why Wersby had died. Perhaps it had something to do with the green folding over 'Associated Adhesives', 'Bee Dee Contracts' and 'Bowber Effluent Treatment', as you turned into Gray's Inn Road. A sudden nostalgia — a sudden green winking summons away — as you passed 'Come Across for the Best Meal you've ever Come Across' and 'Pleased to Meet You. Meat to Please You' and 'Harkness Crush Lighter Effect'. The thirst for green meadows came again as you passed 'Rexine Adhesive Fluids', 'Flow Unit Front Face Plate' and 'Release Ratchet Inc.' on the side of a van. Somewhere fat black bumble-bees hobbled heavily from sweet william and phlox. You saw a stream lulling away into a deep pool of ten feet under some trees. Fishes hung in the water. Foxgloves hung like wild cats' fat tails breaking out in savage spots from which bees were fired. You heard the shush and drop of foxgloves' hoods. A deep mauve shadow inside each one. The pad of the wind through

121

shining trees . . . You arrived at Bude Mansions, but Thelma would be there waiting for you. ('We'll have a glass of sherry. My first drink today, and then we'll just sit and talk about your day and try and make goodness and joy spring up where you thought only all your own negative thoughts had been alone.')

CHAPTER X

'Hullo' Thelma called when you got in. 'A better day? Did the dryness go? Come and tell me all about it, or are you still down in the dumps? I haven't had a drink yet today, so what about one?'

You could see by her appearance and hear by her speech that she had not had a drink. But she only withered you even more and you went straight to your music room and got out your cello. Perhaps if you went back to Charles Hivère and had some more lessons? . . .

'But you must deal more lovingly and more tolerantly vis all zat is in your brain' you could imagine him saying. 'Zis parchedness . . . music exacts its toll and has its punishments . . . And you must learn to accept ze postponement. You are bringing ze tension and ze release home too soon. Here ze composer is lifting you up in surprise and suspense but *le moment de vérité* is not yet . . .'

Your style under him had grown more relaxed and more open. Like a flower it had opened. And you had developed an eloquent, passionate vibrato. And he had taught you to be greedy for participation and communion with other players. You no longer wanted to play alone.

But what would he say to you now? Was it a musician's task or in his range to help break down the thin membrane that stood between you and the music? The orgasm that is almost reached but not quite? Could he help you to break down the thin membrane? Could he help you achieve again that grave but sweet disquiet with matter? Could he provide that tide that would suddenly rise and take you?

And so much had passed since your lessons at Passy. You had said goodbye to Giselle and come home.

Soon after that you went for an audition for the London Symphony Orchestra and were offered a place. It was when you were playing seven years later on the first desk of the B.B.C. Symphony Orchestra – you were already married and had one son – that you had met George and he had invited you to play once or twice with the Tavistock Quartet. You gave a solo recital on the South Bank. You played all Bach's Cello Suites. There were only a few hundred people in the audience but George had come.

'Bless you' he said afterwards and kissed you.

You got good reviews in the press next day too: 'A strenuous style . . . a beautiful tranquil tone . . . a passionate interpretation of that mysterious sad Sarabande . . . A controlled revolt against emptiness and unmeaning . . . a grave but sweet disquiet.'

Then George asked you to join the quartet on a permanent basis. You were delighted. You were becoming disenchanted with the big tones of an orchestra and its big gestures. In Paris you had played in an ensemble and studied Alban Berg's 'Lyric Suite'. You were moved and excited by its controlled mixture of the ecstatic and its falling shadows. You had also studied his Opus 3 quartet. This was your first practical encounter with twelve-tone music and you wanted to play more. But it was only later when you were playing in a big orchestra that you looked back nostalgically to this period of quartet study as though the gestures of the orchestra had become too big and heavy and machine-like. Too rhetorical. You wanted to play music that expressed a whole theme in three pizzicato notes, or which expressed a whole world in the tenuous unwrapping of a nucleic cluster of angry demi-semi-tones. You wanted the comradeship of only a few instruments, a few voices, the Schubert C Major Quintet with its intimate love-dialogue between the first violin and the pizzicato of the cello.

You joined the Tavistock Quartet. You became the quartet-in-residence at Sussex University. You travelled to America and Germany and France. George wanted to accept an

124

invitation to South Africa but the rest of you refused. You had wanted to give a recital for the Campaign for Nuclear Disarmament but George had put his foot down:

'Artists become political only at great cost.'

Spring and the first opening of the year; the spring face suddenly turned on you as you stood on the common with your banners waiting for the march to move off: a Yiddish theatre group in front of you, three ballet dancers, five military strategists, ten M.P.s, hundreds of union branch-secretaries and thousands of C.P. members, trade-unionists, teachers, miners, medical students and housewives . . . Central Hall, Westminster, had been packed last night, filling the hall and the overflow halls:

'. . . Political responsibility is passing from democratically-elected leaders to military ones. Manny Shinwell was Minister of Defence in 1950 when the decision about the Bomb was first made, but he didn't know anything about it.'

'Bullshit. You bet he did.'

'Over £200 million this year for an independent deterrent that may be obsolete next year . . . You could wipe out trachoma in West Africa for the price of one aircraft carrier.'

'But we're not interested in the economics of it' the next speaker had argued. 'Ours is a moral argument to bring about a new kind of world. Unilateralism is concerned with the survival of the individuals who make it up. "There will be millions of survivors" ' she mocked a recent Civil Defence poster. 'Not "would be" but "will be"! . . .'

'Will people at last' the speaker went on after the uproar had died down, 'will people at last refuse to identify themselves with a race or a history or a class, and instead with humanity? . . . The fascination for extinction . . . The lack of wonder and love for life . . . The ability to accept only a doomed, sealed future . . . So many miles of total destruction . . . So many miles of partial destruction . . . So many miles of lethal fall-out. Is there anyone who would want to do this to another human being? A time will come when men will refuse to do this to their brothers and sisters.'

'Now! Now! Now!' the audience shouted.

'Then get up from your knees! Stand! Shout! Refuse the

role laid out for the ordinary men and women all over the world. The role of victims.'

You gathered on the common. The ground was dark and cold with rain, but the sun was coming and it would be fine today. Pools of water shook in every uneven place, and the wind tore your banners, pulling them first one way then another, tore at your voices, blew away the loudspeaker's shouts:

'Motherwell behind Clapton Young Communists. Yorkshire miners behind Woodcraft Folk. Yiddish theatre group, are you there?' the voice came disjointedly through the loudspeaker as you merged into a long column.

The Star of David moved. The miners' huge emblematic banner rose into the wind. Four men tugged at the ends of its stays, holding it back straight in the wind. But it would be fine today.

You had marched all day yesterday in the rain, through grey, flat, drizzling countryside where the only moving thing was the earth foaming dark at the tractor's mouth. Water still hung in the grass. Its blades were still full of rain. The houses and pavements were black with it and your clothes still felt damp. But today a body smell came from the grass when the clouds parted and an arm of warmth reached down to it.

'Convert the Labour Party' a group was arguing.

'Child Jesus, can you get behind Motherwell?' the loudspeaker failed to interrupt the argument.

'Christ! You might as well say convert the Women's League of Health and Beauty or the Finchley Lawn Tennis Club.'

'Yes, the Labour Party will listen to you at election times, but once they're in power they all change.'

'Child Jesus behind South Africa and Motherwell . . . Motherwell can you hear me? . . . Child Jesus are you there? . . .' but the loudspeaker was drowned by the literature sellers' obdurate cries:

'Only a tanner to get you to the heart of things.'

'Only a tanner for all the things they don't want you to know.'

'Yugoslavia for only ten pounds. Ten pounds for ten days and guaranteed no road-building this time.'

126

' "Living against a wall is a dog's life".'

'If you want a decent line . . .'

'We won't get off the ground until we have a decent line.'

'Marchers! Marchers!' the loudspeaker clicked in the trees, sent up a high-pitched arrow of sound that shot the birds from the branches, but was not heard by the marchers:

'Hackney and Islington can you move in behind Spanish Anarchists. Holy Child can you move further back.' A priest in a black cape and cassock rubbed his nose and got the Holy Child into the long column. The march moved forward and stopped, unpicked itself slowly from the common and spread out down the street. A Trinidad steel-band played:

'Like a Tree that's Standing by the Water'

and thousands of unilateralists moved slowly forward, walking, running then stopping, fighting the wind in their banners as they sang in reply:

'We Will not be Moved.'

The march at last lurched forward led by the huge and beautiful banners of the Unions and the black C.N.D. banner:

'Aldermaston to London. Easter 1961.'

Thelma pushed Andrew in a push-chair; she stopped to watch some sheep feeding in a wet field:

'Don't they all look peaky? Their food must taste so cold. But they like eating it standing up, they say. "If I sat down to eat, the food would get caught half-way down and I shouldn't reap the benefit".' Andrew laughed. Thelma was pregnant again and she went home at nights. Julius and Nancy and you formed a band, trumpet, guitar and you on the piano accordion your grandfather had given you. You got lifts to the front of the column and stood there playing as the four-mile march came winding along:

'Oh the Family of Man Keeps Growing,
The Family of Man Keeps Sowing
The Seeds of a New Life Everyday.'

'Ban the Bomb on Wednesday' a man on a bus shouted at you as the bus went slowly past. 'The revolution begins at half-past two.'

'If you think you can do what Disarmament Conferences

can't do' another man shouted through his cupped hands from a car, 'you should have your brains tested.'

'We're unilateralists. We won't wait for them.'

'Get rid of NATO and nuclear alliances.'

'Nuclear bases are nuclear targets.'

'There is no defence.'

'Soon there will be a Bomb that wipes out people by radiation but preserves buildings and property and capital installations. Human beings are expendable. Installations are not.'

'We are the writing on the wall.'

'Ha! Ha!' the man on the bus laughed down as it ran beside the marchers. 'Ban the Bomb. Ban evil. Ban wickedness. Do you really think that by walking along with bare feet and mouth organs you can do what politicians can't?'

'Politicians are caught in prestige politics and nationalism.'

'And anyway, ours is a moral argument,' a girl added half to herself tying up her shoe.

The bus went very slowly. The man leaning out of the top deck surveyed you all. He ignored the trade-unionists, the miners, the middle-aged and the housewives with prams. 'So yours is a moral argument?' he stared at the girls with good teeth holding moral views like the milk-cartons they sipped from; girls in leotards and barge-hats, or Johnny-Boys and home-made trousers.

'No to nuclear alliances!'

'No to using the Bomb first.'

'No to the deterrence myth, the murder budget, the terror strategy!'

'Out! Out! Out!' the marchers cried.

'No more Auction Block for Me' the Trinidad steel-band played.

'No more. No more' you sang and shouted back.

'What about NATO?' a youth in a fast car shouted as he went by.

'NATO can go where Sunday went.'

'It's not on the cards. We'd have the American Marines in first.'

You broke for lunch and lay in the first slight, shifting, tender spring sunshine that unlocked the bark and wood and

mud and gravel and brick and stone till they smelt like water-
ed herbs.

You sat down and relaxed outside a pub where the Holy
Child had gathered.

'It's a marvellous myth' Julius stared at them as they sang
Mass, standing round in bare feet on the damp grass. 'God
coming down a few hundred years ago and being born in a
disused factory or a homeless people's squat. And his follow-
ers liked the stories about him so much that they revolted
when the story-teller killed him off, so he had to resurrect
him. It's a great myth till you get to his wounds healing us
and his flesh and blood for our food.'

'And the sacred heart pierced with swords' said Nancy.
'And no birth-control. And woman being the limb while man
is the head. And the blood and the Crusades and the Inquisi-
tion and the persecution of the Jews.'

'And the Papacy hand-in-glove with Fascism.'

'And the Pope condoning the bombing of Guernica'
Thelma added.

'No. It's a lousy myth. A disgusting one,' you said. 'Guilt
went out with the fear of masturbation and V.D. Nothing like
a shot of penicillin for clearing up original sin. And the God
who came down from heaven a few hundred years ago — and
in the aeons of history this isn't so very far away — came
down to Shepherd's Bush or Clerkenwell Green to Part III
Accommodation — to me this has always been a vulgar joke.
The Hindus have a much better myth' you said, 'placing the
Gods before recorded history began. Christianity shows a
lack of respect for history, dividing us off artificially from all
the great civilisations that existed before this outburst of the
slave-mentality in a world that had just begun to get rid of its
Gods.'

'And what a God!' Nancy exclaimed. 'A God who loves
the stick insects best. The creatures who can camouflage
themselves best. A God who cares about the quantity rather
than the quality of life. Who promises survival after the
H-Bomb first and foremost to the insects that can stand the
heat and the cold and the drought of the desert. Who loves
best those men that can camouflage themselves best; lie down

129

in the desert and become like their environment. Not to quarrel. Not to disagree with the powers that be, however corrupt they are. Lie down and camouflage yourself as a stick or a stone and you will survive.'

'But the God who came down into this "camouflage" farce refused to take part in the pantomime' the Holy Child shouted out at you. They had all finished Mass and were standing in a circle singing:

'Go. Mass is ended. Go in Peace.'

Thelma went into a lavatory with Andrew. 'Don't go into that toilet, love,' the attendant called as she went in, 'a coloured woman comes here and uses it.' A black woman stood there by the mirror beaming and touching up her elaborate hairstyle. Thelma went into the lavatory. When she came out the attendant gave her a filthy towel to dry her hands on. 'From me cubby' she said. 'Best not use the ones you find in here. Coloured people use them, and the marchers.'

'But I'm one of them myself.'

'Still, you look the clean type, not like some of these girls who come in with bare feet and throw their rubbers down the toilet.'

The lavatory attendant came out and stood in her doorway in the sun, shading her eyes and staring at the marchers sprawled over the common. Three ladies in straw hats carrying banners: 'Britewell Mothers' Union says No to the Bomb', stood waiting for the march to line up again.

'The masses of the oppressed Capitalist world rise against their slave masters and Fascist thug-leaders' Julius commented. 'Drop them on Washington. Let's have them to terrify the lites out of the Pentagon with.' He watched them.

Rain came suddenly in small clouds over a pale blue sky. A sudden grey blister opened over the trees. The pines were dazzling with sharp needles as the rain fell. There was a reddening tinge along the horizon. The rain stopped. The sky was suddenly an estuary of red and green, like a truce after a battle. Water was jumping in gold balls off the roofs.

Some medical students came past singing to 'John Brown's Body':

'The feet have started marching and they've
    only just begun.
They're going to put the fear of hell in every
    mother's son.
Aldermaston, Downing Street and Chequers,
    here we come
If you don't ban the H-Bomb now.'

'Better dead than red' a counter-march invaded their columns.

'What do you mean?' Thelma cried. 'Is it better to be dead than be a small power like Switzerland or Norway? Who wants to be a great power if it means four minutes to pray?'

'Watch the people jump' you shouted as the counter-march chanted on. 'Look! They are jumping when the whistle blows. They are jumping, first just off tables and chairs. They can jump higher than that though, the whistle-holder claims. Try. Yes, they can jump off walls and off roofs, and then off the tops of twenty-storey buildings. They are a jumping crowd, and you can see them now as the whistle blows jumping off the Post Office Tower. Or they can lie still and feign death. No, they aren't dead. Just camouflaged and lying quietly waiting till the whistle blows and they can begin jumping again, and chanting as they jump: "The British people are prepared to be blown to atomic dust in the name of preserving the West from Communism".'

The night was a crystal dome. Every sound came over it. Cars, men talking at street corners, an ambulance siren, a child crying in an upstairs room, early leaves stretching against the dark boughs in the wind, and the faint strumming of a guitar:

' Ain't gonna follow war no more no more,
Ain't gonna follow war no more.'

Or sitting by the fire you lit that night, sitting all night on the hard concrete of an empty children's paddling pool, singing, playing, cooking and arguing:

131

'We shan't get off the ground until we start civil disobedience . . .'

'Dresden, Hiroshima, Nagasaki . . . We can't afford to have politicians any more.'

Someone murmured that you were on the brink of a revolution. A Unilateralist T.U.C. A General Strike. A Unilateralist Labour Party. An economic and a social revolution. A revolution in consciousness. People were at last beginning to refuse the role of the girl who has been raped by a drunk in a dark alley and is pregnant with his child. The Home Office considers her case carefully, has her examined but finds her healthy and good for many years' child-bearing. And there is no overpopulation problem at the moment. So they won't consent to a termination.

'She didn't half let herself go at first, poor kid. She didn't want the child' the neighbours would say. But as she grows big with it, she begins to change, make friends with it, and smile, at first a little bashfully, but soon understanding the arguments and smiling over her cotton smock, steering her belly through the door, becoming co-operative at examinations and cheerful instead of angry and hysterical, smiling, waiting for further directions, how to lie comfortably at night with the State's baby inside her, how to breathe during labour . . . smiling and acquiescent as though her freedom consisted in learning to adjust herself to the way things were.

But it couldn't be like that! It wasn't possible that people would accept this kind of freedom. It wasn't possible that this was the form that the second half of the twentieth century would take. It wasn't possible that people who lived in the grey streets you had marched through all day would fail to revolt at this use of their lives. It wasn't possible that they would accept the millions to be spent every day all over the world soon on the fantasy of power and the reality of terror. Once they saw through the deterrence argument, once they saw through the verbiage of roles and responsibilities, independence and autonomy to the evil and useless thrust for State power and individual annihilation . . . It wasn't possible that people would continue to take the female role and watch the marchers surprised:

132

'Too bad, isn't it, Mr Radioactive' girls licking ices at tennis courts were calling. It wasn't possible that people would accept their role in nuclear bargaining: a city for a city, *pair passu* — A million? Two million? — till each side came to realise that they weren't willing to sacrifice more. It wasn't possible that people would continue to accept the female role.

You lay down on the wooden floor of the church hall where you were spending the night. Someone was playing a guitar in a corner. A few people were singing:

> ' "If I had a hammer, I'd hammer in the
>   morning,
> I'd hammer in the evening,
> All over this land.
> I'd hammer out freedom.
> I'd hammer out a warning . . ." '

Tiredness and lack of food elevated you; gave you a feeling of euphoria, an unprecedented happiness. You lay there under the table with your arms round Thelma who was spending the night this year with you in a church hall, hearing people whisper in corners, or argue at the seats in the middle; cooking behind the food-hatch, or practising anarchist songs from the Spanish Civil War in a corner under a red-and-black flag. The whirring of the air-extractor. The sounds of cups and saucers. The creaking of the floor-boards under you. The staring white cups you had drunk from. The piles of dazzling uneaten sandwiches. The smell of floor-boards and dust . . . You lay in Thelma's arms happily and you both slept.

Then there were the Tests, and on television prominent members of the community discussed the latest series. Only a few thousand people lived on the Pacific Islands near where they had taken place, the Minister of Defence defended the government's decision, and the people of these islands were, on the whole, far less evolved than us. And after all, let's face it, more of them would die in the next ten years from drinking the foul marsh waters of the island than would die of leukaemia or other radiation hazards.

'It was, I know, a very very hard decision to have to make.' The Minister put his head on one side and thought for a moment, puckering up his face in a puzzled frown, sniffing and screwing up his eyes: 'But of course it had to be a political decision not a moral one at this particular point.'

Thelma joined the local Committee of One Hundred and sat down in Trafalgar Square as a protest at the current series of Tests. You went to Holloway where she had been sent for refusing to pay her fine. You paid it for her and she was furious with you when you drove her home.

'I'm sorry. But the children. And you know we are off to Scandinavia next week.'

'Is Scandinavia more important than these Tests?'

'Sorry. Sorry.' You kissed her.

'Tests. Radiation. What sort of a future for ourselves and our children even if the Bomb is never used?' Thelma asked your M.P. when you went to lobby him at Westminster.

'Our commitment to the Commonwealth and to the free world at large would be betrayed if we renounced our role' he repeated what he had said on each of your visits. 'We cannot pursue a responsible role in world affairs without having behind us this power to manoeuvre. The experience of the thirties has taught us that to ensure peace you must be prepared at all times for war. Totalitarianism, as we see it, can never be met by turning the other cheek. Faced with the grandiose and expansive instincts of an ideological empire, we must be able to say at all times: "Thus far but no farther." We must show them not only our own determination to remain free, but our absolute determination to keep the free world free as well.'

'Hearts and brains are needed to keep us free' Thelma protested. 'Bombs will only lead to deserts and no freedom.'

'Yes, well, but I'll let you into a secret.' The M.P. paused and looked round at his constituents. 'There was a time, a few years back, before some of you can remember, I suspect, when I nearly put on my duffle coat and went to Trafalgar Square to be with you.' He smiled round. 'In 1954. Around

134

the time of Dien Bien Phu, when Dulles actually had the nuclear bombers out. I almost collected my duffle coat and marching orders and went along to Trafalgar Square. But I think that now we've entered a more responsible era. Gone are the days of "spasm" warfare when you just dropped out everything you had. It's rather like the changes in surgery. At one time you just lopped the whole limb off. But now, new strategic weapons ensure that in place of random slaughter there will be genuine political bargaining.'

'And what is the bargaining price at the moment?' a white-haired lady asked. 'What proportion of the population of this country are you prepared to sacrifice as an acceptable figure for bargaining with after a conventional act of aggression? A sixteenth? An eighth? A fifth?'

Your Member put his papers together, drank some water, and looked at his watch: 'As we've said all along, we don't want to sacrifice anyone.'

'But you must have made some decision about this new style of political negotiation.'

'We don't want to sacrifice a single soul. We want to see the whole nation safe. The Bomb is simply to deter.'

'A Bomb that isn't for use isn't a deterrent. So what proportion of the population would you think it worthwhile to sacrifice in the name of freedom?'

'As I've just said, I think we are entering a more responsible era now and we're beginning to feel safe.'

'We don't march simply because we don't feel safe' Thelma shouted. 'If it was just that we'd be moving to Southern Ireland or joining Civil Defence, and helping with those brown paper sacks they used to talk about, and soaking our curtains in borax, and learning to rub two sticks together for fire.'

'And I ask you,' the white-haired lady added, 'who would want to be a survivor in your hands? With the so-called leaders all underground in their R.S.G.s? And the two systems still going even if there are no actual citizens left.'

'I should say that is coming it a bit strong' your Member looked surreptitiously at his watch. 'Well, I musn't keep you.' He shook you all by the hand, telling you how glad he was that some people still bothered about serious subjects, and how much he respected your consciences. 'And incidentally Madam,' he addressed the white-haired lady, 'the hot-line has opened up new and powerful opportunities for peace. Now that we have this understanding with Moscow that in a crisis between the two great blocks there should be as little misunderstanding as possible . . . If, for example, a missile were launched by accident, we could get on the hot-line . . .'

'And tell them it wasn't meant?'

'It could be intercepted.'

'Or it might not be. Some comfort for the eight million or so people involved to know it wasn't "meant".'

'London could take up to eight H-Bombs and still survive. A single H-Bomb could "take out" an enemy city without a single Allied casualty.'

'And what about when this Bomb gets into the hands of terrorists?'

'The Bomb will be kept only in responsible hands, I assure you. And now I mustn't keep you any longer.'

You left the Houses of Parliament. The streets seemed flat and still in spite of the rush-hour traffic. You saw rows of neat, flat, well-tucked-in hospital beds in a ward with only a hand waving here and there and falling back on the beds' smooth uniformity. These were not the victims of a nuclear war. Nor were these the survivors. These were the victors in a new democracy, lying down and living in quiet terror. You were in exile still, as you had been as a boy. But the Kingdom was no longer a place on a map where you could escape from the beach boys or your mother and be with your 'real' father again. You had, you thought, come through. To the real Kingdom, not the fantasy one.

'And it's deep in my heart,
I do believe
We shall overcome one day'

half a million people sang on Easter Monday after the speeches in Trafalgar Square.

You left the Square with Julius and Nancy. Thelma went

136

home to put the children to bed and the rest of you went round to George's house in Maida Vale without even bothering to change out of your damp anoraks.

Without even consulting each other or using any words you began to play the Mozart D Minor Quartet, K.421. You sat down in the old garage that George had turned into a music room and played as though this were the climax distilled from the four days' marching and talking. The inadequacy of words. The tediousness of language. The words that only covered and hid the abyss. The Mozart was a sudden extrusion into the perfect language. When you came to the Andante you heard people listening outside and moved your chairs out into the street and played in the darkness without music . . . The Minuet and the first violin's eloquence above the pizzicato of the rest of the strings. . . . The bird-like theme of the last movement where the first violin soars up into a theme of persistent joy, a pure flame of love and joy and tenderness climbing into the night.

When you had finished you embraced each other, as your strings had reached out and embraced each other in the dark. You had never played the work quite like that ever again. It was as though a pure distillation, a perfect substitution, a triumphant exchange of darkness for good had taken place between you and the events of the past four days and you were retempered through joy.

You came home to Gray's Inn Road exhausted. You kissed Thelma. You hugged each other. You undressed her slowly and penetrated her. All the tensions of the last four days' marching were released; all the strands of hope cleaned and cleared and straightened and lying in the same direction. You penetrated her slowly, releasing one by one every locked cell, every nerve-ending, lifting them, stroking them, one by one; talking to them, caressing them, converting them till you reached orgasm and she cried out. It was a long moment and then you too cried in relief.

You slept. You woke. 'I'm going to switch the light on' you said.

'No, don't! Let me draw the curtains first. We don't want all the neighbours in Bude Mansions to see a pair of

luminescent buttocks and write to the Ministry of Unidenti-
fiable Objects about the latest weapon.'

You laughed. You kissed her again. You got dressed.

The windows were flung open and the clip-clop of foot-
steps came down the street. The clock ticked on two notes,
G sharp and then a slight crescendo to A. You could hear the
sound that Thelma's clothes made as she got dressed, her
nylons rasping together as she moved. The squeaking sound
of the carpet as she crossed the room. The creaking of Turkish towelling working against her skin. The sound of the
carpet as she crossed the room again. The hissing sound of
paper being torn up. The running water in the tap like glass
splintering and crashing into the wash basin. The sound of
the lock as she opened the door. Two notes, A and then B as
she left the room again. You looked out of the window. It
was a silver steel night with the moon hanging on its back and
the stars huge and bursting down in some kind of greeting, of
salutation, as you stood there staring.

But that was over ten years ago and the Bomb had prolif-
erated and the British had accepted their female, hospital role.
And then there was Vietnam.

CHAPTER XI

'They've got the tears of Christ in alcohol. Lacrimae Christi.' Julius sat in your flat after a rehearsal sipping a glass of sherry. 'And the Virgin's Milk. Liebfrau Milch.'

'All they need' said Thelma, 'is the vinegar mixed with gall that they put up to Christ on a sponge when he cried out in thirst on the cross.'

You thought of one person hanging for sixteen hours by his nailed hands and feet, and given vinegar when he cried out for water. Then there were the thousands of other rebels and slaves and thieves to whom it had happened yearly. How could it possibly be, such pain? You went into the kitchen and held a spoon in boiling water and laid it on the back of your hand and tried to hold it there. You lit a cigarette and stubbed it out on your cheek. How could it possibly be? St Joan? Napalm? It was impossible to think of it happening to one person, let alone thousands. The men and women and children who had to endure unquenchable fire far more terrible than having nails through your flesh — a very easy death in comparison. Or fragmentation bombs splintering through their bodies. A lightheadedness came down on you as you stood at the windows. Such pain wasn't possible, something cried out at you. No, it couldn't happen. Some God would intervene. Or some bodily mechanism. But you knew none did. You lit a cigarette again and stubbed it out against your throat. You felt faint and dizzy under the white hospitaline sky. You could hear their voices screaming from thousands of miles away as clearly as you had heard the nurses screaming during the flying bombs when their hostel got a direct hit.

'Supper's ready' Thelma called. She had been to the butcher and bought half a pig's head. The butcher and his wife had taken an ear each and cloven it down the forehead and nose:

'Lovely bit of meat you've got there behind the nasal cavity,' the butcher had knocked out the pig's teeth with his hatchet and scrubbed its tongue and sponged the hair in its ears and nostrils.

'That little morsel you've got there, Julius, comes from his psycho-muscular tendon' Thelma said. 'And your piece, Will, is part of his nasal cavity.' You pushed your plate away. It couldn't be. The sky outside was white like bone. The trees spread their dazzling green out at you and it winked inside your brain. You looked down at the people in the street. They looked so tender and fragile squeezing between the cars and lorries as they tried to cross. The white-hot sky reminded you of the Second World War and the time you went to South Lambeth Hospital where your mother had been taken.

'But it didn't hurt so much at the time, when they first brought me here' she had kept repeating childishly. Loose skin flapped on her lips when she spoke. She lay there surrounded by tooth-mugs and feeding cups like big white cannons pointing at her. Even the bristles of her toothbrush seemed too much hardness and spikedness for her to bear. And that was such an easy war for you both.

'It can't be,' you stared at the sky.

'An accidental dose of defoliant is almost as bad' Thelma read your thoughts. It seemed a barrier, their pain, that made further talk or thought or action impossible. Your mouth dried up. You went to the tap. Let alone music.

The window-frames rattled as a plane went over. The window panes in Saigon would rattle like that and vibrate every morning as the huge B 52s stood over the city then roared off towards their targets, the jungle, the rice-fields, the villages.

'Two Hiroshimas a week' said Thelma.

'Our boys are doing a great job out there' Julius put on an American accent and imitated the G.I. you had watched on the television last night. 'Thousands of feet above the jungle

140

and watching it grow tame. I guess you get a feeling of power as you drop out your stuff.' The filth of the jungle cleaned up with fire. The vegetation losing its hold over the soil as the defoliants came down. The crops in the fields growing white and soft like Kleenex tissues then curling down to the ground. 'These surgical strikes are sure cleaning out the Gooks.'

'Go and get a coonskin.'

'Ya, you could call it a kinda feeling of confidence you get in Uncle Sam. A good image as you clean up Charlie from out of there,' the serious, blue-eyed, clean-shaven, well-built, milk-and-ice-cream-fed airman beside his buddy agreed. 'When you get up there and see you've got control over thousands of miles of this green garbage muck and Charlie with it, you sure get a good image of Uncle Sam.'

And from the hospitals came the high screams of children that could not be comforted.

They came back from their 'surgical strikes' exhilarated. Saigon was full of them swinging round smiling and round-eyed and huge among the small dark impoverished people of Vietnam; long-limbed, laughing and rangy; round buttocks swinging in and out as they moved round the capital enjoying the life of the boulevards and looking for girls.

For the rich women of Saigon it was fashionable to have their eyes operated on to make them look round and Western like their guests. And there were floods of showers, electric fans and refrigerators, bras and see-through panties imported to arouse interest in Western democracy in the South: to introduce and invite people to the Western way of life. Sugar popsicles, pop-corn and chewing gum for the children, toys for the victims of napalm.

'Your country is on the road to progress. Let's get it going. Let's get up and go. We're on a mighty course in South-East Asia. Remember the parable of Lot's wife and never look back.'

But the majority of the people made no response to this invitation to the new freedom that was being offered.

'Ungrateful gooks. Turn Vietnam into a parking-lot or a ball-park or a massive air-strip.'

'We ought to bomb it back into the Old Stone Age' the

Generals suggested. And the Western press devoted time to discussing what kind of a government in Vietnam the American people would tolerate and what kind they would not, while from the cool white hospitals built and equipped for the inevitable casualties of the 'hearts and minds' campaign came the high, soft cheeping bird sounds of napalmed children on mattresses covered with Disneyland cloth, a continuous even steady cheeping sound that does not expect to be relieved; an agony and a loneliness that does not expect to be reached.

'It is our prayerful wish that we can bomb them to the conference table.'

Sometimes you had minor successes in your campaign of protest. Resolutions were passed at Labour Party G.M.C.s; resolutions were passed at T.U.C. and Labour Party Conferences, urging the British government to dissociate itself from the war. But the government ignored them.

You tried to raise money for the victims. You gave your blood. You gave money to raise enough for an anaesthetic unit needed in Hanoi for removing mother-bomb splinters from the flesh and organs.

There were marches and vigils. There were days of fast. You heard about Song Mai from a French-speaking Buddhist monk in Paris whose relatives had died there eighteen months before the news reached the American press. But newspapers refused to publish your evidence. 'Only another anti-American atrocity story.'

'. . . trying to save a helpless dictatorship from their own people' Noam Chomsky wrote. 'And now there is Song Mai or Pinkville. More than two decades of indoctrination and intervention have created names like Pinkville and the acts that may be done in a place so named. This is no isolated atrocity but the logical consequence of a war of extermination directed against peasants. "Red" and "Dinks" and "Coonskins". America has institutionalised even its own

142

genocide. The world's most advanced society has found the answer to a people's war. To crush it they are obliged to eliminate the people. This policy puts America at the moral level of Nazi Germany . . .'

And in February of each year, at Tet, you received New Year Greetings from the Provisional Revolutionary Government of South Vietnam. It was always a silk-screen printed card thanking you for all your support during the year and the picture they had sent was not a bomb-crater or a mattress with one survivor on it from Song Mai or a mass grave or a pile of scorched rice like black clinker. It was of a girl pouring water over her buffaloes, or a woman in the rice-fields, or a child in a boat with a fishing-net, or a boy with a wreath of white flowers in his hair.

'Marchers, can you hear me?' the voice from the loudspeaker came down from the trees as you assembled at Turnham Green. 'Quakers, can you get behind the Anarcho-Syndicalists? Holy Child, can you finish eating? Eton College, can you move in behind Holborn Office Cleaners? . . .' A march struck up to a Revivalist hymn-tune:

> 'Leave me Yankee man leave me.
> Leave me soldier-boy, leave me.'

'Stories, all the stories' came the literature-sellers' cries as the march moved forward. 'Only a tanner to get you to the essence of imperialist wars. Only a tanner for all the things our government thinks we have no right to know. Only a tanner for an analysis of our government's assistance to the U.S. in this war.'

'Drop some napalm on you, I would' a bus-conductress swung on the platform of her bus, staring as the long column trailed past. You leafletted her bus:

' "U.S. Quit Vietnam" ' her cross-seat passenger read: 'I agree. The Americans should get out. They are a disgusting lot, these Asiatics, and they don't deserve American help at all.'

'Why can't they just mind their own business?' the

conductress leaned out at you, puzzled at the banners made of windproof gauze that you had evolved over the marching years; the posters that were waterproof; the seats that folded and went into the pocket; the torches that stayed alight in rain and wind; the stickers that didn't need spit; the leaflets that stayed in a pack; the portable latrines that blew up; the lollipops that weighed only an ounce. The conductress stared down her leaflet-strewn bus:

'Now you get a broom and sweep out what you done to that floor. I've got three straight runs to the Tunnel and I'm not going to wade through all this muck for three hours, am I? . . . Who do they think they are' she stared still puzzled as her bus moved on. 'Saying we won't have this and we won't have that. Why can't they just mind their own business?'

'U.S. quit Vietnam' you shouted.

'Quite right!' a man in a straw hat applauded clapping. 'Bravo. Well-marched, marchers. Keep it up!'

'Yes, it's about time someone brought a bit of morality and humanity into public life.'

'Morality!' a newspaperman roared at his stall. 'Don't make me laugh.' He pointed at some girls in white velvet plus-fours with bells at the calves; girls tinkling on dulcimers slung round their necks:

> 'I'm gonna lay down my sword and shield
> Down by the riverside . . .'

The song wandered down the long straggling column from one town to the next: 'I'm gonna study war no more.'

'Harmless, that's what we are' a student beat his head with a rolled-up newspaper. 'Too damn nice by half.'

The man in the straw hat was still clapping: 'Bravo marchers! Stand up and be counted. This is a sickening war.'

'Do you know what?' the student watched him. 'C.N.D. has tamed us. We've become as harmless as the "Sallies" selling *Warcry* in the pubs on Saturday evenings.' You could march and shout as much as you liked. Worshippers coming out of church would see balloons rising in the wind:

' "U.S. Quit Vietnam." '

Children would run after you to catch them. Churchgoers

would smile as the steel-band went by. Children in scarlet caps and blazers with Latin mottoes on them would cycle round you, and girls with pigtails would run home crying:

'Mummy, do tell Julie she can't have it.'

The sound of lawnmowers. The sound of electric mixers. Washing-machines running and the squeaking of swings. And all the time the world's greatest power was destroying one of the smallest and poorest . . . 'a small country whose gross national product' the Secretary of Defense would rally doubters, 'is smaller than that of a one-horse, Middle-West town.' They weren't going to be defeated even if it meant turning the country into a parking-lot . . . And your balloons floated in the air 'U.S. Quit Vietnam', and children ran after them and caught them and men in straw hats cried:

'Well done, marchers!'

'C.N.D. has tamed us' the student cried, and a counter-chant ran along the column:

'Victory to the N.L.F.'

You felt only light-headedness and a feeling of disrelation as you marched along with your banner hearing the chants:

'Out! Out! Out!'

'N.L.F. In! In! In!'

as if these shouts could have anything to do with the napalm, the B 52s and the half-a-million American troops. You were silent, as though words had lost their meaning. But silence couldn't water the letters of the alphabet till they brought about peace. Where were the words? Where were they hidden?

'Shepherd's Hill Says No.'

'N.L.F. In! In! In!'

'And where's the working-man?' someone shouted.

'He knows he's a victim just as much as them. And he's making the revolution where he should. On the factory floor. The masses have got their own patterns of leadership. They don't need a lot of C.N.D. do-gooders telling them what to do.'

But the cry went up again: 'Where's the working-man?'

'He's not here because he's seen through us' a bald-headed man with ginger eyebrows bawled from the top of a lorry. 'He sees us for what we are. A lot of Liberal, Social Democrat do-gooders who don't really want to see the N.L.F. take over the South. They just want America to stop bombing the North and withdraw her imperial territories back into the South. Imperialists at the head of this march, Out! Out! Out!'

'Out! Out! Out!' the marchers replied.

'Ignore diversionary tactics' the leaders of the march boomed through loudspeakers. The man with the bald head bawled back:

'Those who don't want to be taken over by the imperialists at the head of this march turn left at the next set of traffic lights and go as far as the school where there will be a true analysis of this war.'

'Keep straight on, marchers' the loudspeakers replied. 'Keep straight on to the lunch-break. Ignore diversionary tactics.'

'Ignore the bourgeois leadership. Turn left at the traffic lights.'

'Keep straight on.'

'The C.I.A. is operating at the head of this column. Just siphoning off your anger. Come to a meeting where a real rationale will be given. That's the only way we'll get the working-man with us.'

'C.I.A. Social Democrats out!' he was cheered. The march split. The futility of protest.

When the Easter marches had been massive and Trafalgar Square was packed on Easter Monday in 1961, '62, and '63, the newspapers ignored them or played them down as a Communist Front or a load of mealy-mouthed middle-class pacifists or a lot of 'carefully dishevelled exhibitionists'. When the movement split over non-violence and again over Vietnam, the press laughed at the violence of the 'pacifists'. When the anti-war demonstration in Grosvenor Square grew violent in 1968, they looked back nostalgically to the great days of C.N.D. when a 'massive conscience had overtaken the country and unilateralism had seized the imagination of the British people'. Now you felt you were a puppet mechanically taking part in some charade.

You would come in after teaching or rehearsing and go leafletting with your local peace group in Exmouth Market,

Chapel Market, and Leather Lane.

'How are you, Handsome?' the costers would call.

'No better for seeing you, Tragic. Here come the peace people.'

'We're all with you in this. It's a disgusting war' a woman with a face like church candles took some leaflets and spread them out over her stall among 'True Danger', 'Sex Without Love', 'Sound of Battle' and 'Smoke of War'. 'I've voted Labour forty years, but I shan't no more.'

'Liven up, ladies!' a coster was calling a little further along. 'Just the thing for your toilet, Myrtle. Here comes Mr Napalm!' he called out to you. 'Only thirty-five pence for this toilet spray. Make you fresh as a daisy again. Not got a toilet, Mr Vietcong? Here's a gentleman hasn't got a toilet. No, sorry, Mr Megadeath, the toilet comes separate. You'll have to go up to the Council for that.'

You handed out your leaflets: 'No, thank you. I've had that one before.'

'You should take a boat and go to Russia.'

'You're Communists. That's what you are,' a fat, squint-eyed butcher wagged his finger at you. He had stuck signs at random out over his browning meats: 'Home Killed' he slapped on some ox-kidney tightly-knit like grapes; 'Sure To Please' he patted a sheep's heart with a white lardy casement round it; 'Full of Blood' he had hung on a drawn hare that swung above you dripping. You had a sudden déjà vu. You knew what was coming next: he would pat his meats and his signs and the woman at the stall would say:

'Half of buttock, please Stan. It's only for the dog.' The butcher would slap down the meat and look at your leaflet: 'Now what I'd like to know is have you ever been in the Army? I was one of the Desert Rats and I got to know what these oriental people are like.'

He hauled down a carcase of lamb from a hook in the frame of the stall and swung it upside down. 'Best if you get at her upside down' he winked and his wife simpered as he laid the carcase on its back and hacked at the hard white lard enfolding the kidneys. You knew exactly what he would do and the sound as he tore back the stiff starched layer of lard

147

round them, cracking it open like a nut and popping the soft shining liquid kidneys out with his thumbs: 'Now have you ever been in the Army? You answer my question and I'll answer yours.'

You handed round pictures of napalmed villagers. Half a dozen photographs of rush-matting. Some had charred people lying on it. Some of it covered the dead. There was a dead child beside a dead ox and a child with a bicycle pedal blown inside his thigh. In the background were the remains of a village that had quarrelled with its headman about the use of the communal well and the chief had reported that the Vietcong were there and the planes came over the same evening.

'. . . chopped cheese and blowing his nose out on the pavement' voices came down the lane . . . 'Strip poker she played every night although she was pregnant . . .' 'Three people's work I did and I buried my father on Tuesday.' They stared at the leaflets and the pictures:

'I've seen that one. I've seen it on the telly.'

'. . . Fatty passed to skinny and skinny passed it back.'

'Yes but what can we do?'

'Where was the goalie when the ball was in the net?'

'Yes but what can *we* do?' A woman had tears running down her face as she asked. You no longer knew the answer to that one, if you ever had. And you could not play.

You stood at the top of the market while a C.P. member shouted through his tannoy: 'Who are we to tell a people thousands of miles away what kind of a government they can have? The Pentagon wants to bomb them to their knees but this time it won't work . . .'

You had lobbied your M.P. 'I'm with you on this issue' he had agreed. 'But what can I do? A backbencher who protests against this war is regarded as an outsider and an extremist and the things he says are taken with a pinch of salt. My voice can best be heard if I remain a moderate. We must draw attention to the inexpediency of this war and the fact that America doesn't really need that part of South-East Asia.'

You had circulated petitions. You had gone door-to-door round the tenements to get signatures:

'I'm with you on this. All out.'

'Not interested.'

'I've had that one.'

'Mum says if it's the peace people tell them no.'

'I'm just about fed up with all this Vietnam. Vietnam.'

'Is it for them or against them?'

'You've got to keep these dark races in their places other-wise they'll be swarming over the world.'

'Vietnam. Vietnam. What a lot they give us to worry about these days.'

'Right. Good. It's a filthy war' an old-age pensioner pressed a florin into your hands.

'Atrocity stories' a man shaving at an upper window in Georgian Wilmington Square cried down: 'When have there ever been wars without atrocities? The North should be pre-pared to negotiate.'

'Did we negotiate with Hitler?'

'The North is callous in what it expects its people to bear. Let them come to the conference table.'

'Did we say that to Hitler?'

'The Americans aren't Fascists yet. Look at all the dissent inside America.'

'And look how dissent is treated. What about tear-gas and the Kent State shootings.'

'The State Troopers over-reacted there. All this anti-Americanism. Is it just because we lost the Second World War?'

You went down Chapel Market on Sunday mornings:

'That's my daughter on the Costa Brava' a man was show-ing photographs to people standing round the whelk stall eating. 'On the Costa Brava, but I couldn't get all the details.'

'What do you want all the details for if she was your daughter like you said?'

'. . . Then he must know Brummy. Lives at Walthamstow.'

'Three days I waited in for the chiropodist. Worked there ten years. Did three people's work. Buried my father on Tuesday, and now they don't want me back.'

'. . . And a really nice pair of fur boots. Not the kind that goes all thin and tatty after a few months.'

'. . . And the home-bather didn't come neither.'

'. . . Lives at Walthamstow. You must know Brummy.'

149

'And the car didn't stop . . .'

'So she said to me: "Don't sit next to me, you slut with a cold".'

'. . . Haven't got a shop-steward now.'

'Here comes Mr Radioactive again. What's it about this time, Mr Megadeath? Free corsets for the over-fifties? Passion-killers for the blind?'

'Terror's what they need to bring them to their senses.'

'Loads of reading. Be in time.
Bags of stories, thrillers, crime'

the man at the second-hand book-stall shouted mechanically. Old ladies' dresses, blouses, ash-blond wigs were lying by a suitcase on the pavement. Old people stood round them turning them over. The mechanical chant came from the second-hand book-stall:

'Now there's your Plains to the left. And your Romances to the right. And your Down-to-Earths are under the counter.

"Reading public be in time,
Spend a sixpence. Spend a dime".'

And from a stall piled high with toothpaste, shampoos, shaving lotions and Durex gossamers: 'There's your shampoos. There's your toilets. And over here is your Ethicals.'

Their faces as your déjà vu came again were half-familiar. And you knew exactly how the man would lift his beer off the Durex, put his money in the leather bag under his apron and repeat: 'And there's your Ethicals.'

An old woman stooping in the gutters for fruit and vegetables fallen from the barrows took your leaflet with trembling hands:

'Is it for them or against them?'

'It's for them' a lady boomed behind her in a deep voice. 'We're all for them, Mrs Andrews. And how are those feet behaving today?' She smiled at you but refused a leaflet: 'In a moment I shall be completely loaded down with bits of Guide Uniform. But' she raised her blue eyelids, 'you have my moral support.'

'Veet-nam' some children followed you down the market.

'Monkey-faces.'

'Monkey-face yourself. Valerie's going to pluck my eyebrows for me.' You could no longer play.

You walked through Islington pushing leaflets through letterboxes of old crumbling Victorian houses where shadows stood behind front-door glass panes. And when you inserted the leaflet, your fingers would touch the cold bony fingers on the other side greedily sucking the leaflet through the tight sharp narrow jaws of the letterboxes. You climbed stone steps with crumbling urns at their sides, up to front doors where the shadows waited for you. You went down the steps again. At the bottoms in the damp areas old men stood watching you climb down and touched your arm slightly.

'You haven't forgotten me, have you, chum?'

Or: 'Was it me you were looking for, gov?' whispering, stretching out their hands for the leaflets greedily.

Or: 'You missed me out, son.' The voices quavering, the thin white lizard cold hands snatching at the leaflets then dropping them. A group of old men and women would surround you:

'Was it for me . . . ?'

'Read it out to me . . .'

'Tell me what it says. If it's the Pools, then it's been a long time coming, it has.'

'Read it out then. I haven't got my specs.' But you had not got the heart to.

Then there were twenty of them standing round you waiting for the seventy-five thousand, crowding round you, panting, shuffling, stretching out for the hand-bills and petition you carried round in the twilight, blinking water from their eyes, wiping their eyes with scraps of screwed-up paper, moving their dentures up and down:

'Is it a gift? . . .Is it a free coupon?'

'Read me what it says' an old woman in a flowered apron with a huge brown tumour on her eye came at you. Knotted, gnarled, bony fingers with swollen joints came at you snatching the leaflets. A woman with an umbrella hooked a pile off

151

your arm and the old people swarmed round her grabbing them up from the ground. Mouths made gabbling movements. The woman with the tumour shook her eyes clear of water:

'It's only me eyes . . .' They seemed to crowd round you from everywhere. They seemed to grow out of the damp brickwork of the basements. They surrounded you but they made no signs to each other.

'That's right. Let me have what it says. I knew my luck would turn up one of these days.'

'And nice and clear please. I'm not deaf but I do like a bit of clear speech.'

You choked. You could not bring it out, what you had come about.

'Just read out what it says' someone from the back shouted impatiently. The old lady with the tumour snatched at the pile again and they spilled on to the drain. The crowd round her moved to pick them up. She lifted her dentures up and down. Her eyes guttered like candles, eye-water dripping on the leaflets. They were all shaking:

'Read me what it says.'

'I'm sorry. I'm sorry.' Your voice shook. You gave the old lady some money and went away. She looked at it for a moment, snoggled and screwed it up in her wet handkerchief and fumbled in a plastic hold-all at her feet:

'What a lot they give us to worry about these days' she sighed. 'First it's Vietnam. And then it's Biafra.'

'And now there's this spaceman in trouble up there.'

The President of the United States was smiling and ordering more 'persuasion' bombing. There were photographs of him in his pants and vest because he had lost another two pounds in weight this week. His weight was down. His blood-pressure was down to that of a hale and hearty young man and he was saying:

'It is our earnest and prayerful wish that we can persuade them to the conference table.'

August Bank Holiday and the telecasters thought they saw signs of strain on the holiday-makers' faces as they made their way to their favourite beaches. But as the day wore on, expressions became more relaxed. The trippers seemed to be enjoying their ices and candy-floss and hot-dogs as they lay in the sun or queued for the Big Dipper and the Arcades. During the afternoon, however, there was a brief rain-squall and they rushed for shelter and joined in community singing organised by the local Women's Institute . . .

August Bank Holiday and you leafletted the people strolling in Finsbury Park. Two girls stopped to stare at the photographs of a woman who had had her legs blown off by a mother bomb, and the napalmed children, their bodies dark and bubbly with burns.

'The left one looks like our Jean.'

'Get away. Our Jean isn't a black.'

You watched them wander away licking ices and queueing to ride in the little fibreglass boats on the lake, and queueing to have their sunburn treated at the St John's Ambulance van.

A freak hot bank-holiday. You could hear the little boats chugging round the lake. The air was misty and white. You felt light-headed again. 'The scientists engineer the destruction of the world while the social scientists engineer our consent.' And having accepted that role for themselves they could not but acquiesce in the destruction of Vietnam.

You saw a great hospital before you, and the patients lying still in their white beds. Only an occasional arm wavered down the long ward to show they were alive. But you were there too. You were lying among them. You had become acquiescent and dead, and could not play.

'You despise ordinary people' Thelma accused you when you got in.

'And myself too. The bird Eneke-Dhota said: "Since man has learned to shoot without missing, I have learned to fly without perching." So we must keep flying. Mustn't land or perch anywhere. Must cast off all belief or feeling for that is dangerous and will lead to unfreedom.'

'I think to me it's a kind of challenge.' Thelma put her arms round you. 'I want to get a job on the assembly-line and

153

get to know exactly how it feels to come in exhausted and emptied and be expected to feel politically and humanly when you've been dehumanised all day putting blobs on chocolate cakes or counting bits of paper up to a hundred, or lying on your back kicking a lever. Now if we could give them a proper link-up with their own experiences,' you felt thirsty. The tree outside the window pulsed out at you. The green winked and called you down, 'maybe the working-man sees through us, sees us as a lot of middle-class do-gooders . . .'

'You've read Erich Fromm. We've been freed from want, but no one knows what we've been freed for. "Destructiveness is the outcome of the unlived life." '

'Destructiveness!' Thelma cried. 'It's we who are just as destructive as the Americans. Pity is destructive!' She stood miles away from you. Her lips moved up and down. 'It's destructive just to pity the victims instead of taking sides with them. No one went around in 1936 mumbling about pity for the Spanish Republicans. They said: "Let them win. Let the legitimate government win. Let's go and fight and send them arms." Victory to the Vietcong!'

'They will win,' you said. But the feeling of light-headedness came over you again. Voices came from the trees outside:

> 'If thou canst get but thither,
> There grows the flower of peace.'

'Vietnam is ruining my work' you cried. 'I haven't the time or the emotional energy left to think of Vietnam any more. You must go to that demo alone next week. It's not just the time. It's because Vietnam keeps breaking into my music. Not in a fertile way that C.N.D. did. But as a cry of deadness and exile that music only increases. It stops me from playing. Something all the time interrupts me and comes between me and what I'm supposed to be playing. I can only play mechanically with my tongue in my cheek. And all the time, inside, I'm dead. As an artist, how can I not take sides in the struggle? But how can I take sides with people who would put me to silence if they were in power here?'

'It sounds as if you are in silence already.'

'People who would prevent me from playing "Formalist"

music that has no popular theme or social appeal?'

'It doesn't affect Julius that way' Thelma said wistfully. 'He is committed to military victory and it makes him play beautifully.'

'Yes, but I'm not Julius. My emotions have been eroded by this war. I only feel light-headed and empty and dead. You must go on Thursday without me. I must stay behind and try to find my roots again. Though I don't know where to start looking for them. The arts can't assimilate such a terrible thing as the napalming of peasants in the rice fields. I feel when I'm playing that I'm in a prison cell with only one small crescent of a window in the ceiling to let the sound out. The sound doesn't come out' you shouted. 'The sun doesn't shine on me. I am dead.'

'It's a sort of constipation? . . .'

'No, a sort of exile from the things I love. "I see nor feel how beautiful they are".'

'War imposes exile.' Then: 'But the N.L.F. are winning and we shall be at peace again.'

'A victory for the schematised life.'

But it wasn't just that you were lukewarm about the coming victory. It was that the war had taken away your inner space. You were burnt out. You were walking to the cutlery drawer, drying a knife and dropping it in. You were hanging the tea-towel carefully where it had hung before but all the time you were separate from these actions. You were watching yourself.

You went into the music room and picked up your cello. You sat down and watched your feet spread out and your knees clutch the cello. You watched your right hand drop on to the bow, the bow drop on to the G string, and your fingers extended, playing an arpeggio. You thought of tomorrow's rehearsal. You looked at the music. But your mind was filled with dry rusty cog-wheels, old bent tins, wet nylons, torn rexene cushions, blown condoms and codeine tablets rubbing together in your mind.

You started to play the Beethoven you were playing at the Queen Elizabeth Hall next week. You watched yourself playing, and Coleridge's 'Ode to Dejection' came to you:

> 'Work without hope draws nectar in a sieve,
> And hope without an object cannot live.'

The sound of fibreglass boats chugging round the lake came to you. And the bank holiday crowds. But they were suddenly transferred, displaced by the trees outside the window. They seemed to be spreading down the road to Offenden and Happenden, and the river bending away into the green, taking you back to the Kingdom. A homecoming. You gazed out. The doorbell rang. Thelma put her head round the door:

'Paul to see you.' Paul, a member of your peace group, danced in.

'Mr Parrish' he lisped, wagging his finger, 'what are we going to say to the British black?'

'I'm afraid I haven't thought that far yet.'

'I know. That's just it.' Paul shook his bush of ginger hair out of his eyes. He lowered his bulbous eyelids. 'That's just it!' He raised his finger accusingly: 'We haven't thought that far. No wonder we aren't off the ground yet. And in the meantime, he's just opted out. He's gone. And we're to blame. Can't you see that if we just stand there week-in, week-out in the lane shouting out that nice Americans mustn't bomb poor Third World people because we feel sorry for them . . .' He stood behind the settee leaning over it and pointing his thin finger at you: 'We've lost them. The immigrants. They've just opted out and gone. And why? Because we haven't given them a proper rationale of this war. Tungsten and tin. That's why America is in Vietnam. Colonial exploitaiton. And that we've never made clear.'

'The Americans want more than tungsten and tin.'

Paul shook his head: 'Tungsten and tin. That would make the blacks in this country see the real nature of this war. They would see it in relation to their own history and the way they continue to be exploited in this country. And we, we can't raise a finger without revealing ourselves for what we are: white men controlling the Third World.' He pulled out a massive typescript document from his pocket and unfolded it. You heard its pages rustling dryly. The wind

156

blew the net curtains at the window. The wind seemed to come from Happenden and Offenden.

'I'm trying to practise' you said faintly.

'Bourgeois music' Paul reminded you. 'You and your class have bugged the masses.' He leaned over the settee. 'You want America to keep its foothold in South-East Asia.'

'I don't.'

'You do at heart. At heart we are all the unpaid agents of the C.I.A. Now this document . . .' The pages rustled loudly.

'The N.L.F. will win. I must work.'

Paul giggled and turned on his heel and played with the tassels of the lampshade and whispered softly to himself:

'Bourgeois music. The music of reassurance and destiny. Making the world feel safe for the middle classes. Making them feel good and on top.'

'You are turning Vietnam into a game.'

'It's you who have already turned it into a game. The liberal bourgeoisie exercising its rights to pity the Third World.' He tip-toed to the door. 'But I mustn't disturb you' he giggled again and was gone. You felt the cool wind on your face. You heard the waters running. You cried out against words but no music came to take their place as it had once done. Nothing came but the sour smell of herrings being soused by Thelma in the kitchen and the sweet coconut smell of traffic-exhaust from the street.

'Supper's ready' Thelma called out as Paul left. 'Success?' she asked, 'if you see my drift.' She had been drinking again.

'Yes' you stood up and shouted. 'All we've got to do now is to bring the country round to the Marxist-Leninist way of life and get the Minister of Defence to ban the Bomb before Christmas and end all nuclear alliances.'

'And did he say whether he would later consider switching the country over to an anarcho-syndicalist way of life?' Thelma shouted too.

'He was all in favour. At Christmas, he said.'

'Good. And did he send any messages for me?'

'Wait a minute. Yes he did. He said "Does she realise that I nearly fought in the Spanish Civil War and nearly sat up all night putting the world to rights with Simone Weil?" '

'Liar, he doesn't speak one word of French, if you see my drift.'

'No' you shouted. 'It was all done by moral gestures of which, you will be pleased to hear, he thoroughly approves.' You looked out of the window. The street looked flat and two-dimensional, like a painted theatre back-cloth, and in front of it the green rose beckoning at you. Thelma smiled at you. She came over and tried to kiss you:

'Feeling better? Feeling more cheerful?'

Tungsten and tin and Thelma hitting a large fawn moth with the washing-up cloth. You suddenly felt faint again as the moth lifted its heavy wings in an attempt to wobble and flutter away. Thelma lunged at it with the mop and thrust it into the bottom of the basin of water. You got a cup and drank cold water:

> 'If thou canst get but thither,
> There grows the flower of peace.'

'Feeling better?' You looked away from her. She stretched out and ruffled your hair. You didn't want her to touch you. 'I must give you more love.' You felt that love was the last thing you wanted from her. She bent over you and kissed your forehead. 'This obscene war.' Her breath smelt of barley wines. 'This barbaric war.' The words only brought back the feeling of light-headedness:

'Why not "Zuleika"? Why not "Rhodomontade"? Any other words would do just as well. Would mean as much. "How the Queen rules",' you shouted. ' "American praises local Guide group". "Who makes the best cup of tea, the Army or the Navy?". "Does Miss World deserve the title this year?" '

'Well, what is there except words? How shall I express my anger then?'

'No one's interested in your anger.'

'Why can't they just let the Vietnamese alone to get on with their lives?' she hiccupped, 'if you see my drift.'

'Please don't go on like that. It does no good.'

'I only have to mention the war and you go all limp and non-violent and holy as though you were the only one who

158

felt anything.'

It was soused herrings for supper. You opened your fish. Two white evenly-shaped lobes of white roe popped out hard and firm. A thick blood-shot branch ran through each of them, breaking out into scarlet tree roots and scarlet branches. You stared at the shining roes, the crimson heraldic tree prophesying war and more war. You pushed your plate away. Tungsten and tin and does Miss World deserve the title this year. You waited for music to come and take the place of words and things. You waited as an insomniac waits for sleep, waits to be picked up and carried away on a tide of sleep. Lifted and carried back to the 'Isles of the Blest'. But the words as you say them only lower you down and drop you back sharply where you were in the yellow dawn with the early birds screaming.

There was another ring at the doorbell. You opened it. It was one of Thelma's neighbours:

'Will, what *are* you doing? About Vietnam I mean. I came to prod you and Mrs P. To get you activated again. Have a sweet. Have a good honest barley-sugar. With none of these synthetic sugars in it. Barley-sugar will give you back more energy for world affairs. Wake up!' she smiled. 'Buck yourselves up! Both of you. We simply must get control of things. The people. Vietnam. Footpaths. Whole foods. Preventive medicine. Macrobiotic diets. Does Will ever go out at night, Thelma? Would you both like to come and meet Oh — Oh what's his name? — And that beautiful village. Where we all mean to go walking one day. Well, what are you both doing about the world? Would you like to be secretary of the United Nations? We desperately need one. My good friend Billy Busman — Or do I mean my friend Dr Clagan? — Anyway, have another barley-sugar. Bad for the teeth? Oh no. I've had no trouble with my teeth ever since I went to Margery Locklease and had my vitamins balanced up. What do you eat for breakfast? All-Bran? That tears the lining of the stomach. Wheatgerm and yeast is the only sensible diet. Probably that is why you are both so inert politically. You lack vitamins and energy. Why can't I get you involved and stirring?'

'We've worked for years for C.N.D.'

'C.N.D.? What is that? Is it anything to do with the old lady who has the dog with the very noisy bark? If so, I want to tell her that that dog is being spoiled with kindness. Nutrition. That is what it needs. But what is C.N.D.? Oh, disarmament. Well I've been in favour of that for more years than I care to remember. Now I've come to prod you. Do you ever go out and do things? Political things? World government? Protest? Will, I wonder if you could help me. This is what I've really dropped in about. I want to know what the colour of the N.L.F. flag is. I can remember my grand-daughter having a very pretty N.L.F. carrier-bag. Blue and pink and gold, I think it is. Blue and pink and yellow. And I want to make one for myself. I'm sure it had a pretty yellow stripe and we want to do everything we can to support them out there.' She turned towards the door. 'Disarmament! The United Nations! We must make all war illegal' she suddenly shouted. 'Just cut it right out,' she banged her fist on the table. 'A poster parade can be very effective, even if there are only four of you . . . No response? I daresay it's vitamin imbalance.'

She went. You shut the door. You raised your hand to hit Thelma:

'Never mention Vietnam in this flat again. And never let your peace people come in here again. Why don't you get yourself a job since you are so under-occupied?'

'Yes, I must get a job' Thelma said quietly. 'I must have worthwhile work. If I can't do anything for — for Vietnam, if you see my drift — then I want to be among ordinary people. On the assembly-line. In the pressers' room.'

'If ever there were another war' your mother would say in 1936 as fog crept into the living room and night trams came howling round the bend at The Horns. 'If ever there were another war' you turned the gas-taps up. The reek of gas and the little Ideal Boiler standing upright in its corner and the reek of burning serge and the woman with the torn ear-lobes sitting very upright with a fly on her eyeball as the tram conductor turned the tub-seats round at the end of the run, and a child lying a little way away from her right arm and her

160

right leg, and the blue night trams chained together and whining away...

The sky was a pearly white, a bone white, a bomb white. Its forehead dazzled you. Its eyes were the winking trees outside in the churchyard gardens. You shut your eyes. You heard the sounds of a departing train running away there where you wanted to be. Then there was silence.

Thelma was in the kitchen. You could hear her above the running tap opening another bottle of barley wine, and Happenden came back to you, flooding back to you over childhood, wreathing you in its green foliage, summoning you back across the shimmering water meadows threaded with shining buttercups and meadowsweet and down to the still brown river where you had once gone with your father when the big children were at school. There would be pink hawthorn petals floating gently along in its drift. The cows would be standing under the great elms that held the evening's drift. You sat there the whole evening just staring at the map that your mother had given you in the Oval Tube Station during the blitz, just staring at Happenden and Offenden and Bligh Woods and Pound Common. It was a dangerous way and yet you treasured its promise. You even forgot that night to unscrew your bow or put your cello away.

You dreamed that you were with it in a long hospital ward. Your hands were too small and weak to turn its pegs and tune it. But you knew your father was somewhere here in the hospital and would do it for you, and you woke calling for your father: 'My music!'

That was over a year ago and Thelma was still trying to get work. She rarely mentioned Vietnam now except to say once:

'Saigon has fallen. The Yanks are scrambling out.'

'Saigon has been liberated' you corrected her.

She was drinking heavily. She would start drinking as soon as you left the flat in the morning and when you got home at night the place reeked of barley wines and she would be flat out on the bed, 'having a little rest'.

Then you had gone down to Julius's at Thorley and she had come back happy and animated and without drink:

'Julius makes me feel real again.' And for a moment you

161

were relieved till she added: 'And we're going to try and pull you through. No one is a natural recluse and I'm sure you aren't. Remember the great days of C.N.D. when we sat all night in the empty paddling-pool. You and Julius and Nancy and me. It's just that you have lost your confidence in yourself and other people and we are going to help you get it back. We all suffered during that war. But it's over now and I'm going to get you back out of that shell, back to your old commitments.' You drew away from her embracing arms and the river floated in, 'or we might go to America or Germany, and you could play in an orchestra there.'

'Are you a London jam-maker?' was written on the side of a passing bus. 'Actylene Carbide Company' on the side of a lorry. 'Jones Sewing Machine Oil' . . . 'Highly-Inflammable Correcting Fluid'. A boy drifting down the road had 'Auto-motive Spring Service' stamped on his T-shirt. There was burning serge in your mouth and hot plasticine, and the arm of the river was beckoning you:

> 'My Soule there is a Countrie
> Afarre beyond the Stars.'

So after the rehearsal you go to John Wersby's flat and collect the original manuscript of his string quartet. You sit in the churchyard gardens looking at it and turning again to the last movement thinking of the black man in Cafford Square and listening to its faraway tonal tune. Gradually the voices of the men and women on the benches round you grow further and further away:

'They'd of sprouted too soon . . .'

'Had French windows and a lovely garden, but there was only the dog.'

'Went through the kitchen floor.'

'One in the morning and two at night . . .' The voices go on but you are no longer there. The music comes and you are crossing the meadow with your father and suddenly the birds are shouting:

> 'Can there be any day but this,
> Though many suns to shine endeavour?'

They are calling you to the river. The clattering birds are calling you there:

> 'We count three hundred but we miss.
> There is but one and that one ever.'

First just the misty childhood water meadows full of king-cups and cowslips and tall silver-white grasses like shining scar tissue and you walking through them with your hand in your father's till the meadows stop and the river is there, still and broad and you a small boy singing and banging your feet in the hard, caked mud of its banks when the big children have gone to school. And your father is sitting down lighting his pipe and the voice comes:

> 'Into my heart an air that kills
> From yon far country blows.'

The wind is hovering over the trees. The cows are sheltering from the sun under the faltering poplars, and the early-morning river runs deep, the elms mounting guard over its solitude. The close-packed leaves are layered with black, a velvet black ignition of soil and air working up above you, and in sudden arrows and flashes and gazes it comes to you sitting there, the deep brown somnolent river and your father smoking his pipe:

'Is it very deep?'
'Very deep.'
'Would you reach the bottom?'
'Not here.'
'Not if you were standing on mother's shoulders?'
'I might then.' And the sudden gaze penetrates you:

> 'And He leads his children on
> To the place where He is gone.'

The gaze goes.

Flatburn Foamtrol is being sprayed under the benches in the garden by a man in shorts with a big red face and red knees. He pushes a hot metal trolley with rubber bonding and parched rubber tyres. Starlings lift and drop bacon rinds flung down for them there by an old lady with a brown paper bag. Starlings on the asphalt with grit and fat in their beaks, and then the gaze comes again, first just the woods smoking with bluebells, then the river moving heavily round the hill:

> 'Oh how I long to travel back
> And tread again that ancient track!'

A starling in the churchyard is eating a feather. It struggles as it hangs half in, half out of its mouth. As one end goes in, the other fluffs out. A starling is struggling to eat a piece of parched cloudy grey plastic. The wind blows a piece of paper at you. It wraps round your legs — an Everseal Neophrene Coated Anti-Static Wrap. ('Send my roots rain.') A streamer of bus tickets winds itself round the benches' legs. The wire waste-paper basket is full of cotton wool smeared with lipstick and cream. (Assessment of activities of daily living. General Mobility. Self-Dressing. Bathing. Food-intake. Sixteen billion tons of T.N.T.)

Smokey bacon appendix flavour; aspirin water soup; Polyfusor air; sterile non-pyrogenic closed circuit output; the volume infused in millimetres.

> 'Such pearl from life's fresh crown' the river erupts,
> 'Fain would I shake me down.'

Shadows are folded in the dense green of the chestnuts — shadows of a necessary death. And when the wind tilts them, the big spinach leaves back and part and mouths are open and waiting to absorb you. You almost expect to see rims of this green around the roof-tops, along people's windowsills, across the hospital, down the fronts of houses and threatening to burst the hard dry streets. You expect to see it triumph in the palms of men and women holding out, instead of money, this cataclysmic green invitation.

'Look! See! You cannot escape it.'

164

'You cannot escape it' the Wersby tune repeats. The city curls up, crumpling like waste paper waiting to be tossed into a bin, and the bad gaze comes again, and the Wersby tune, beginning like a church hymn but becoming something ancient, pagan, far older than churches and Gods: 'Dawn comes on this ancient world to take you . . . Then die, Bride! Die!'

CHAPTER XII

Thelma was running the bath. She stood there naked beside it. A pair of knickers and a bra were lying on the laundry-basket. She tossed them into the water.

'I'm sorry' you said over the thundering of the taps. The taps seemed huge like guns firing off. 'We must both try harder to give each other a little licence to exist. I'll try harder not to erode your morale. I'll try to be less boring in public. And more myself. And you must try . . .' But the taps' huge works drowned your words. Thelma threw another bra into the water, then a grey handkerchief, and got in and lay there with the round end of the squeegee mop resting in her navel, swiping it randomly over the walls, rubbing at the pale grey bathroom dust that had gathered there. The mop waved over your head. 'We must try to make each other free instead of poor.' Splashes of water hit your face like glass.

'We'll get you out of this rut' Thelma said.

She lay in the water swinging the mop to and fro from her navel. 'We'll have people in like we used to do. No one is a natural recluse.' A crab spider with long hairy legs was driven from its home behind the lavatory cistern and she poked at it with the mop. The spider dithered, moved forward then back. You got out your handkerchief to pick it up and take it to the window, but it seemed too large. Its legs would hang out of the handkerchief. Thelma banged it with the mop and watched its legs struggling in different directions, then withering together and shrivelling into a knot. She got out of the bath and scrubbed the spot on the floor where the spider had been till a dazzling circle of green appeared on the dark

166

lino.

'I can't see why you don't get some nice West Indian woman who lives in the Buildings to come in during the week and help clean the flat' you said as you watched the original colour of the lino and the walls reappear after her assault.

'We'll get you back' was all she said. You felt small again and shrank, like the spider, into a shrivelled knot.

'I can't see why you don't get a West Indian woman in.'

'I wouldn't want anyone, let alone a black person, to come in and do my dirty work for me' she replied. 'I'd feel too ashamed. Too colonial.'

'She might be glad of the money and it would be some company for you in the mornings.' The water was noisy. Your voice came small.

'I'm not like that. You still don't understand what I want.'

Thelma rubbed at the walls for a bit longer then she got out of the bath and stood at the mirror staring at her pale green eyes and her long dark wet hair. Her thighs shook as she dried herself, lapped together like two underwater plants. Her knees had big chins. Her navel was sunk into her stomach flesh like a stone plopped into harbour mud. Her nipples were like two corks bursting out of bottles. She stood by the mirror towering over you, the hair under her armpits and between her legs about to smother you, her face no longer waiting for excavation and fulfilment.

'We'll get you back' she said. 'I promise you.'

Then you saw the crab spider unravel itself on the floor, kicking vigorously with its legs. Each long leg had three joints which extended and contracted with a bolt charge. You panicked at its size and lustiness, and put a coffee tin over it, surprised that it would fit, expecting the spider to walk away taking the tin with it. Thelma was still standing at the mirror drying herself and shaking out her long wet hair:

'First we'll invite Annery and the Stolzes. Annery might be able to get you into a really good orchestra again.'

'Or I could take my grandfather's piano accordion and go and play in the "Pindar of Wakefield".' But your voice came out a croak.

It had been Thelma's birthday a few days before you went

167

down to Thorley, and you had given her some scent.

'Very feminine' she had smelt it on her wrist. 'Very exciting' she had tried to sound feminine. '*Femme*. Who can explain her *mystère*, if you see my meaning. If you get my drift.' Then there had been a click at the letterbox. The postman stood there with a parcel for her, a present that your eldest son had ordered for her from the Oxfam shop, some Indian sandals that were too narrow for her, and a little Moroccan leather purse which was too small to take more than a few coins which spilled out when she closed the purse and held it upside down. 'Women love dainty things' she had said, twisting the garnet round to the front of her finger and fitting the matchsticks in. But now she pushed these little pleas aside, the scent, the sandals and the purse, and wrote in the grey scum on the side of the bath: 'non-male'. 'Still never mind' she said cheerfully when she had done it, 'it's your problems we must concentrate on now. My own seem peripheral in comparison.'

'I can only solve them alone.'

'No. Together. With me. I drank and went away from you and didn't give you enough love and support,' she put her arms round you. You were buried in the hair under her armpits. 'But now we are beginning again. Do you think Annery would like the Stolzes? I promise I won't nip into the kitchen any more and drink barley wines while you are pouring out the Montrachet.'

You went to the window and looked out into the churchyard gardens.

'Perhaps Julius will come today' Thelma called out cheerfully putting on a long dress. 'And we'll get to work on you together. Get you whole again.'

You looked back into the churchyard gardens. Coltsfoot was blooming between the wire springs of some rusty bedsteads propped against a hospital shed. Ox-eye daisies popped up among broken abandoned chairs. Upholstery bloomed out of them in a new vegetable mass waiting to be taken up and transformed into green by the engine of May. A thin black stem grew out of a pile of sweepings, sending out a long purple flower, and white pear blossom reared up, Everest

168

upon Everest. I seemed to reach your window and as it rose you could hear the Wersby May morning tune come frighteningly near and loud and clamouring in your brain. You banged some loud discords on the piano to drive it away.

'I must be off now' you called to Thelma. 'I shan't be in to lunch.'

You packed your cello and music and the John Wersby manuscript and took the lift down to the street. The ground-floor button seemed to jump out at you before you pressed it, big and black and shining and leading into the guts of Bude Mansions.

The traffic outside roared at you. The kerb seemed steep. You dropped down off it with a bang. Your cello hit the ground. The island in the middle of the road was a climb to reach. Your cello was a great weight. The Victorian houses and Edwardian Mansions towered over you; the stacked newspapers outside a tobacconist's shop were about to topple over and down on to you.

You turned into Theobald's Road. The railing of Gray's Inn gardens towered over you too. Your head was under the daisies inside, and the blades of grass had long black shadows, sharp like swords running towards you. You were so near the ground that a spot of oil on the pavement bothered you — a huge deep puddle you had to negotiate. The dark lines between the paving-stones were muddy rivers you had to step over. They stretched as far as you could see.

The street grit cracked noisily under your feet. Some men passed. Their feet scooped into the pavement grit and up at you. Down and up and sending dust into your mouth, while the turning bus-wheels rose up over you like Ferris wheels. You could hear trouser legs flapping all round you and the squeak as women's heels rubbed against the sides of their shoes. And you were down there among them watching them twist the grit into odd patterns like lunar landscapes.

A tall green lamp-post was being erected in a deep hole in the pavement, and the red clay soil round it sprang out at you and clawed at your eyes and dazzled you. You passed a café. The door was propped open with a huge cardboard box labelled in big black letters that stood as high as your waist:

'High-Vacuum Carbon Suction Unit'. Some people were eating inside. They looked down at you from tall tables and ate egg and chips and wiped their mouths with serviettes that they threw down at you, paper shadows passing over you with lipstick on them; a bird's shadow covering you; at your feet an oily rag, a mountain at which pigeons tore. And all the time the Wersby tune came down at you from the trees miles up in the sky: 'Then die, Child Bride. Then die!'

You were late when you arrived at the Gordon Hall. They were waiting for you. George was playing his melody from the Beethoven Cavatina. Nancy was repeating a row of fast staccatos. Julius was eating yoghourt.

'Annick has left me,' he reported. 'She was really a rather naughty, delinquent girl. Will Thelma be in this evening, Will?'

'Yes, she's looking forward to seeing you. But I shan't be, I'm afraid.'

You began with the Beethoven Opus 130. Your cello felt too big for you. It slid between your knees. The pin kept slipping. You played each note like a bobbing cork on the top of water, and when you tried to found them securely, to tether them to the phrase as a whole, your mind was on the rafters of the hall ceiling climbing up above you and sending down on to you the Wersby May morning tune. You tried to get inside the Adagio. You tried to get inside your strings, but each time the tune came a rasping sound came from your cello as though a child were repeatedly stroking his finger down the side of a taut stretched balloon.

'What art thou up to, Will?'

You banged savagely at your cello to drive the tune away. 'Sounds like crunching sand' you said, losing the meetings and departures of the first movement. The quartet was fighting rather than playing. Their bows driving to and from you; their hands like crab spiders, their fingers clawing as they drove in and out of the strings, and above the battle, like a cry of surrender, came the tune.

'Canst thou not eliminate that nasty kick?' George was asking Nancy miles away. 'And you did promise to go through that alternative fingering before this morning.'

'Sorry, but I had to collect Basket from the vet. And the

children get out of school at twenty to four and I had to go and collect them.'

'Where's your baby-sitter then?' Julius was asking. 'Where's your *petite garde-bébé?*'

'She burst into tears at breakfast yesterday morning. *"Pierre ne m'a pas écrit"* she kept sobbing. Then she announced she was leaving. She caught the next train to Paris to find Pierre.'

'Look, shall we get on? We haven't developed this slow upward cello unfolding yet. Let's go back to Bar twenty and get those minims in the second violin more solid. And let's be nicer to that delicate wooing phrase at the end of the decrescendo. You sound as though you were trying to drive the cats away, Will.' You were trying to exorcise the tune.

'Don't you think' Nancy thought, 'we are playing this movement rather like a game of Snakes and Ladders . . . sliding glibly from beginning to end without nourishing the development, as though the movement were held together by paper-clips and hair-pins.'

'And this change of key is surely a hint for some repose on my part.'

'And Nancy, can't you try this fingering?'

'I can't get it. All I get is a sizzling sound like fried eggs.'

'And less passion. Less of the Apocalypse. This, after all, is only a very nice phrase, a sort of coda taking back everything the music has said, only in a very well-mannered way. Will, art thou with us?'

'Let's go right through it first' George suggested. 'Then we'll start on the shitwork.'

The Adagio opened with its solemn hymn-like tune but George called at you as you played: 'You're not just supporting here, Will. Let it sing.' And in the diminuendo you blurred a staccato B that should have locked the strings together and your *poco crescendo* faltered as the Wersby tune came again. You were all of you tense and raced through the Presto feverishly, anxiously, buzzingly, like a dentist's high-speed drill, racing to the end, betraying all George's high elated cries, all trying to get there first till George stopped you:

'I can't hear myself feel, you are buzzing so.'

171

Throughout the Andante the cello's delicate bouquets to the strings were not presented. The Danza alla Tedesca began serenely, George leading in his sunny way, but then you started to hug the movement to yourselves, afraid of touching each other's souls and finding only salt there. Then you came to the Cavatina. You played your two *sotto voce* Es then the tune came again as if from another room. George put down his bow:

'Oh please, let's stop. Let's not do that to that beautiful Cavatina. Let's not play such noble and great music in Cambridge next week.' He wiped his nose. He was weeping behind his glasses. 'We aren't. . . We're like souls in hell fighting for their lives. Shall we play the Mozart D Minor "bird" quartet instead?' He looked meaningfully at you. 'The K.439?'

You all agreed.

'Right. Let's break here for coffee and when we've had it we'll start to take the John Wersby apart.'

You undid your bows and drifted into the hall's little canteen to make coffee. George turned to you:

'Do you think we could think in terms of getting the cello into a less supporting role?' You nodded:

'I'm sorry. I'm feeling a bit dead and preoccupied today.'

'Ah, well. We all have our dark nights of the soul.'

'Have we decided when we're going to give this concert to raise money for Vietnam?' Nancy asked. 'They still need the money for their hospitals even though they've won the war.'

'I thought we had decided not to tangle with politics?' George replied. 'Everyone knew last time that the money went to the Vietcong.'

'The money is and always has gone where the bombs and napalm fell' Nancy retorted. 'And anyway what do you mean? There's Julius and Will and me in favour of giving this recital. You are in the minority, George.'

'No. Will is with me' said George. 'So it's half-and-half.'

Nancy looked at you: 'What's come over you?' They all seemed so big sitting there opening their mouths and letting their tongues work over words, while their throats pumped down the hot coffee.

'I've no feelings at all' you said. 'I feel like a flea.'

'I daresay we shall all feel like fleas after a couple of hours with the John Wersby.'

'What about the Grosse Fugue?' Julius was asking. 'Are we going to play it in Sydney next month?'

'If we ever get to Sydney' Nancy shrugged.

'Why shouldn't we get to Sydney?'

No one liked to say.

Julius opened his mouth and put it over the top of his coffee cup and gulped coffee in. Then he shook his face as though he were a dog shaking water off it:

'George is right. It will not do. We can't play the Opus 130 at Cambridge.' You finished your coffee in silence. You went back to the hall and tuned up again.

'Didst thou have any success at John Wersby's flat?' George asked you. You brought out the original manuscript. They all leaned over it, correcting their photostated copies.

'So that is a G natural . . .'

'And that is a D sharp . . .'

'And that pause is in 3/8.'

'At least when he pees on you each in turn there seems to be a kind of consistency and progress in it' George yawned. 'Sadistic as it may seem.'

You sat round and began to unpick the first movement and put it together again. It began with a nucleic buzz from the violins, a cluster of dotted staccato demi-semi-quavers which slowly opened out into an arch into which the cello slowly rose in a long crescendo from its bottom C to its top G. There was a pregnant pause then the strings opened again and the cello rose again sombrely and joined the viola in a slow downward drop to another space capsule.

'Wersby would blithely tell us we could eat all the toad-stools in his forests' George wiped his glasses. 'But I suspect he would be very handy with the stomach pump afterwards.'

'Oh George, you are a philistine' Nancy protested. 'We've only just started to unwrap this and you are off again about modern music.'

'But this could never express young love.'

'You want *Girls' Crystal* for that. Or *She*.'

173

'Or the coming of spring. Or the depths of human suffering. It's like a cat that has been thrown into cold water and drags itself out and all his fur is stark and staring and pointing in different directions ...'

The viola was playing a knot of clustered demi-semi-quavers which it offered to the first violin who undid them, rounded them out, presented them to the cello who inverted them. There was another capsule of silence, then the two violins took up the inverted theme, and contracted it back to its first original nucleic buzz while the viola took up the cello's first sombre rising crescendo, rising up slowly on five notes then falling back into silence; rising up on six notes then falling back, the original theme sadly but firmly taken away.

You put down your bows. Even George smiled slightly. ' "Man was born to suffer as the sparks fly upwards." That is a lovely phrase, that *piano,* clean off the bow, but let's get that silence more shaped and rounded. It's a beautiful silence, but we are playing the three bars that lead up to it like knitting. Let's go back to Bar ten and work up that crescendo then pause, crescendo then pause. Then I think the viola takes up the theme with violence. Don't you think so, Julius?'

'There is something certainly there,' Julius hummed. 'Shall I never see you again, oh my sister Fox, the Night. When the frost is on the bough; when the leaf is withered ... But listen to this.' He played a gentle sudden enquiry in the viola line and the cello daintily picked up half the notes and reproduced them with another pause capsule between each one. An answer, then another gentle enquiry, then a blessed dropping and falling off and away into silence.

'That's nice. Let's encapsule it. Let's surround it, making it denser and denser till the viola is absolutely squeezed out into its rather lyrical adagio.'

Julius shook his head as you played. 'That last phrase has become a flat and lifeless drop in tone colour. Let's try not to sit down on those last two Bs before the opening staccato comes again. La-la' he played.

'Can't we make that G flat rounder and fuller?' Nancy asked. 'Give it a middle as well as a beginning and end.'

'And to use a new bow there, Nancy, is about as sensible as

trying to get head first into your trousers.'

'And let that A bloom' George hummed. 'Like a cottage garden in June.' Nancy grimaced.

Your cello had come back to you. The A bloomed on your bow. You practised the grave disquiet of your long rising crescendo leaping into a high orgasmic cry in the thumb position. Then Nancy came in with her downward drops in thirds and fourths and there was a pause capsule.

'Coming' said George. 'Let's just look at the second movement now to see how it connects.'

The next movement was unexpected, like a good dream coming after a bad day. Like a murmur of reconciliation after a crime. Like grace and laughter instead of anger and retribution. It was the viola's movement, playing a long legato theme in a framework of semi-tones sparkling like stars. Then you all burst into a Milhaud-like carnival of the human spirit, a sudden theme of gratuitous joy.

'The only true response to the quiet society of the Bomb' said Nancy as you played. It was a hurdy-gurdy tune of light-hearted happiness. You began the movement again:

'Like wandering at night when no one is about' said George. 'Like seeing the world freshly after snow has fallen. Not bad.'

'It's coming.'

You smiled and felt the cello between your knees and the bow sinking into the strings and watering the bare notes on the page as you delivered the violins from their original agitation and thrust out a row of well-rounded minims, then a capsule of silence, then the gratuitous cry of joy.

You felt your size come back. And the miracle of human hands working, shoulders, wrists, elbows all in comradeship and harmony as the hurdy-gurdy theme broke out, at first a little rickety, uncertain, wobbling, then straightening out to the final climax. You all laughed and put down your bows.

'Let's break here for lunch and come back after to undo the last movement.'

'I'm tired of ploughman's lunches' Julius said, 'in noisy pubs. Let's go to the Trattoria and drink Chianti and have Fegato alla Veneziana.'

175

You turned into Theobald's Road. The sun was shining on the beautiful Queen Anne houses in Great James Street. The planes were lighting up the street. There was a warm smell of sun on brick and plane bark, and you could see the children from St George the Martyr School going in their gym-shoes and T-shirts to play rounders in Coram Fields.

Pink blossom fell on your hands. The shadows of the trees and the wrought-iron railings of Doughty Street made patterns over the street. Pink geraniums stirred gently in window-boxes. The city's sights and sounds and smells excited you as you felt the warmth of the sun on your hands. A worn old lady at an upstairs window was watering her window-box. The water fell on the street in front of you like music.

You went into the restaurant. Nancy was telling George about some recent visitors she had had.

'You are very intolerant,' George sighed. 'We are all at the mercy of each others' adjectives. Why aren't you more loyal to your own sex? Women are so treacherous about other women. Why aren't you more Women's Lib?'

'Because I don't believe that sexism and the oppression of women is entirely the men's fault. Women are the first to will themselves and their daughters into the sexist role. The simpering female desire to please comes straight from mother. Women on the whole like it that way and men only exploit what the female starts. It is women who corrupt their daughters, the married woman who sets the attitude towards the spinster. Men only connive. It is women who have made themselves as mindless as possible at the expense of their less fortunate sisters. Mind you, I don't exclude myself from that. But it is from their mothers that girls learn not to do anything that will spoil their chances of marriage. And women today still think they are unfulfilled if they have no husband or children. No one would accuse a man of that simply because he had not married.'

'Casual sex' Julius yawned. You ordered food and Chianti. 'Long live the Pill. Have the same man twice and you are in danger of becoming a member of the establishment. Why did you fall into the trap of marriage?' he asked Nancy as she munched at the salad on her sideplate.

'Just weakness. And my mother, I suppose. Being a musician wasn't enough for her. And the guilt of not feeling fulfilled, I suppose. However much nonsense that may be. My own immaturity and lack of courage. I didn't get married till I was twenty-seven and my mother was so anxious about my future. Placatory guilt. That was what it was. However it was my own weakness as well as my mother's.' She spat saliva at Julius as she emphasised the words. 'Sorry' she said.

'Not at all' said Julius. 'I like other people's saliva.' He licked where she had spat.

'Women would liberate themselves in a blow without having to burn their bras or break up Miss World contests if they would live in the objective world.'

'Or play Lysistrata for a bit.'

'Or that.'

'What nonsense' Julius interrupted. 'It's when women begin to take a look into the outside world beyond their uteruses that male aggression and anger and prejudice come down upon them hardest. Look at Marie Curie.'

'One day there will be a pill for everything' George looked up from his food. 'We'll give Nancy a peace pill so that she won't eat her heart out any more about sex or Vietnam or the Bomb. And her playing will return to the serenity and vigour it had before she started getting so bugged up by it all. Then there will be sea and sunshine pills for Julius. Blue seas and hot rocks and cicadas in long dry grasses and the smell of thyme and basil and olive groves.'

'I don't need a pill, thank you.' Julius sipped his wine. 'Life is good enough for me as it is. And what pill for you George?'

Nancy looked at George venomously. 'We must put George on L.S.D. so that he sees flying toads and lizards the size of articulated lorries. And sees his thumbs the size of the whole world just as he is about to play the Cavatina. And everything turned inside out.'

'And a green world where man is no longer the master' you spoke for the first time.

'And napalm pills' Nancy added, 'so that he sees the horror of it all.'

177

'Yes. George needs L.S.D. He needs to be unnerved for a bit. To see the world in a less orderly way.'

'His pill would end in disaster. He would start playing the Cavatina on the double-bass. Or get the illusion that he could fly out of a top-storey window after a couple of staccato Bs.'

'And what about Will? What kind of a pill for him?' Once they would have offered you Nancy's peace pill, but now they were silent.

'Will needs a youth pill to make him twenty-five again.'

'No let's give him Praed Street and the Harrow Road on a hot afternoon in June. Then he would play as he used to.'

'I'm playing the Harrow Road already' you said. 'I've been playing it all the time, only my cello no longer takes off from there as it used to. What I need is a great river, a great tide, a great wave to run over me and drench me. Or a pill that would give me back my feeling of inner space.'

There was a moment's sympathetic silence. Then:

'How is Thelma?' Nancy asked as though she were changing the subject.

'We all need pills except Julius' Nancy finished her wine and wiped her mouth. 'This quartet will soon turn to sand.'

You went back soberly to start on the last movement of the Wersby quartet.

'Let it fly like a bird' George sang when you got back to the Gordon Hall. 'A bird on the wing. A blackbird beating its bounds at twilight.' You looked at the score. There was silence. Nancy scratched her head with her bow. Julius was nodding over some semi-quavers.

'What do you think I should do with these? They come in the first movement and again in the third. And in the second violin, don't they, Nancy?' He leaned over her manuscript and went on playing to himself. You lit a cigarette and propped it up on the windowsill. It seemed immensely high up in the wall. You had to reach up and get your cigarette down. Ever since the conversation about pills in the restaurant the Wersby May morning tune had been with you, and now as you picked up your cello it was as clear as though it were being played in the street outside. You started the last movement. Your cello gave a noise off its G string like water being splashed into boiling fat.

The last movement began with a knotted cluster of demi-semi-tones repeated from the first movement, then they opened up into a broad lucid viola theme, six notes in a musical shorthand that was read back, expanded, interpreted with comments from the rest of the quartet: 'Ah yes.' to each other's statements, and 'But surely', 'If it were', 'If it might be'. Then suddenly you all four burst into strict fugue. Then it was inverted on the viola and the rest of the strings started to cluster thickly again as they had done at the opening, but instead of the long slow legato crescendo there was a silence and the music suddenly became tonal, in the key of A Major, and you broke into the ecclesiastical chorale of the May morning tune.

At first it just spoke of elms spreading into the misty warmth of the early morning; fields where horses and cows huddled; hedges full of cow-parsley and vetch; ditches smelling of warmth, of chickweed and nettles and a new life spreading out at you, gazing out at you in the early morning as you lined up in school and went in procession through the village and up to Rackham's Manor beating the bounds with your sticks and chanting of the new life gazing at you in pink hawthorn and blackbirds stuttering over the still grass.

'A lovely theme' said George as the tune wound along country lanes and down the water meadows. 'Let's get it right. Let's bring out that lovely *piano* and make the audience strain for that last phrase. That's a lovely phrase, full of expectation and promise, and leading into . . .' But the tune didn't stop at the cantabile. As you went into its fifth phase it overturned the morning salutation to the spring and a thunder came from the cello and words burst out from your head, a dark green May haemorrage over you thunderingly, pouring from the trees:

> 'May moveth all in white,
> But for the room,
> A cross in roses dressed,
> A torn departure.
> Roses' rims ringing

Thy shut mouth,
Thy departure's ease,
So near but nevermore.'

'Sad!' George put down his bow. 'This should surely be the second movement leading into the life-affirming hurdy-gurdy carnival dance.'

Julius was repeating his part tersely, cutting the tune down to its barest detail, cutting out any hint of rhetoric or decoration, sucking in his lips and making chewing motions with his mouth as he always did when he was absorbed in a musical problem. 'So he killed himself' he said at last.

'I am coming to you' his playing said. 'I have come to you. To take you where your father went.' You tried to play with him but the music came to you loudly from outside. 'If thou wouldst see me then, then die, Child Bride, die!'

You stood up and unscrewed your bow.

'It's coming, Will. It's coming.' George wiped a tear from his eye. 'It's sad but it's beautiful. We must work at this tomorrow. But we shall have to break here as I'm recording at five.'

You got up but the music came at you again and hit you with a blow that made you turn and look for some assailant. By the river they were dressing your father for the May rite and he was weeping as they buttoned him into his robe, standing there with his chin up and his legs apart, and the river running slowly behind.

You packed your cello and said goodbye and turned back into Theobald's Road. The buttercups were shining among the delicate white unfolding lace of meadowsweet. The bluebells' smoking grey shimmered from the darkened woods. Pale pink and white hawthorn leaned over the water, the birds criss-crossing its shade. You were drawn along smoothly by the tune as if you were on wheels. It drove you from behind and drew you from in front, suctioning you forward, up to the neck then floating down to that place the tune spoke of that was not death, not nullity, not terminus, but fulfilment ...

'When May comes with bands of flowers

Pray that her passing will be swift.
For wedding is in her,
Her bride awaiting,
And she too sure will be
Thy end to wreathe.'

You turned into the Gray's Inn Road still dragged onwards by the tune.

'Hullo' Thelma called out cheerfully to you. 'I've been spring-cleaning the flat.' You went to the piano and banged out some harsh dissonances to drive away the tune.

'What do you keep doing that for?' Thelma asked.

'Just a little tune that keeps coming to me and I try to drive it away.'

'What little tune?'

You went back to the piano and banged out some Prokofiev.

'What little tune?'

'It begins like a tune we used to sing on May morning when I was a child, walking round the village and carrying bunches of flowers up to Rackham's, the big manor house.'

'But doesn't it bring back happy memories then?'

'The tune changes to a horrible message.'

'What message?' You said nothing, trembling on the side of the chair. 'What message?' Thelma repeated gently, coming close to you and sitting beside you and stroking your hair. 'Please tell me what it says.' You were silent. 'One does like to have some idea if one is to help one's husband and give him proper sympathy and support. Please tell me what it says' She kissed your forehead and gently drew back your hair. 'And then perhaps the tune will go away. Please if you love me, tell me what it says.'

And when finally to get her off your chair and to bring her caresses to an end you told her:

'It is a message of beauty bound up with a message of death. Of finding. Of completion.' But you got no further. Thelma slid off the chair and stood there upright and angry:

'What morbid nonsense. Art isn't morbid. And what an insult to me and the children. Death is nothing but oblivion

181

and nothingness.'

> ' "Into my heart an air that kills
> From yon far country blows." '

'How cheap and vulgar. What a cowardly way out. Just because you are in a dry patch. And what a travesty of all the good things that music should tell you. Music tells us how to triumph over life and suffering and Vietnam. Even my little knowledge tells me that. And think of Strauss's Four Last Songs. Think of your Opus 130.'

'Don't.' You blocked your ears to block the sounds of the tune out.

'How wicked that music should tell you a cheap thing like that. To believe that!'

'I'm not asking you to believe anything.' You rocked your head backwards and forwards with your ears blocked. She stood there with her arms open as if to say:

'Come to me. And the children. We are life. Even if it is only in a small way. And music is life.' But you didn't bother to respond to her. You walked away and she followed you.

'And this dryness of yours. It's only temporary. We'll all go away this summer and make sand-castles and do silly things like that. We'll go back to your village in Sussex and have picnics and not think about music once.'

But the hooded sullen gaze came to you again. 'A faithless and betraying land' you cried. And yet you treasured it. 'Oh help me! Why can't you help me?' But that was the last thing you wanted. Your head was light. The trees in the churchyard gardens were reaching up to draw you into them. The pear tree was yearning up.

'I'm just going out' you said. 'Julius will be here soon. But don't wait supper.'

'Just try to make the link-up' Thelma was calling after you. 'The link-up between that beautiful tune and the new life that is in front of us. Now that I've stopped drinking. Now that I'm here again. Now that this hideous war is over. Just make the link-up.'

CHAPTER XIII

It was almost twilight when you climbed down from the train on to the high wooden platform of the station. Birdsong came like leaps of water forced up from cracks in dark rock. There was no one about. A single star in the sky gave you great joy. You felt even closer to the ground. You walked up to the village feeling the warm embrace of sun-soaked cottage walls on your face and hands. The air smelt heavily of cut fields and hedges and moist ditches. A lamb gave a solitary cry. Blackbirds were sliding silently between the fat white daisies of the cottage gardens, and you were under the daisies' heads, under the blackbirds' wings.

The cut grass lay in grey ashes. You were among its strong green roots underneath. The smell of cut grass, the sour smell of the hawthorns, the warm smell of tarred roads, and a small crescent moon with a sharp edge clarifying the evening blue sky . . . And all the time the May morning tune called you on, drawing you, sucking you, driving you through the lanes of the village, past the Norman church and the school.

The thrushes stood in the churchyard under the yew trees and among the tombs. Little pale white flat flowers like Communion wafers dropped on to you from the plane trees as you walked. White blossom hung above you in spiders' webs full of snow. You passed the cottage where you and your mother had lived so uneasily. Purple was bleeding out of the green bush by the front door, and from the twilight singing of the birds thick buttercups and cowslips seemed to spring in the meadows around. You were drawn through the village by the tune and passed the end of the beach road and up the lane where the signpost stood with meadowsweet and cow-parsley still growing up round it . . . 'Happenden and Offenden' . . .

You remembered the lane, the place where the beach boys would ambush you; the place where you had found a fledgeling fallen from its nest, a raw young blackbird broken naked from its shell and dropped tailless and wingless and screaming, its mouth open the width of its body and you were thrusting sticks and pebbles down its red open throat.

You remembered the lane but you had never gone beyond the sign post before except on that visit remembered from another world with your father when the big children were at school. You had always stopped at this stile and never wandered alone over the watermeadows and down to the river except that time you found him standing there, lying there and beckoning you away with him.

The lane became a track. Your head felt light. You felt drunk from the call of the tune. It drove you on. It extruded you. You were so close to the ground that daisies dazzled you and the meadowsweet and vetch sprang up behind your eyes and ears. You were so near the ground that you could hear the insects creaking, grasses being bent and displaced by ladybirds, and the fluff and crunch of plane seeds under your shoes. You were so near the ground that a fallen twig became a rod pointing to the place where you had to be.

There was a drumming in your ears. The trees thrust down at you in loving suffocation. The birds called you to the land. The buds of lilac were unfolding down on to you to draw you in. And the music came again:

> 'But when you have caught her in her green
>   design,
> When she has gazed on you,
> She will throw her strangling ropes round you,
> Lily bands to whiten your neck as they close
>   upon you,
> And buttercups' dazzle to bind your closed eyes.'

You turned the bend. The great lobed brains of the chestnut tree sprang on you. In the beginning was the Word, and the Word was made green flesh and the Word sprang upon you. You came to the great oak tree stump where you had sat with your father:

'Let's pretend that this is my little residence.' You came to the river where your father was lying. You were so near the ground that the dandelion clocks were milky white domes waiting to crash in the wind and you could hear their splintering sound as they were broken open. You were so near the ground that you could see that the green-mauve bags of the shepherd's purse each held a drop of rainbow dew. 'Can there be any day but this?' the music seemed to sing.

The river was narrower and weedier and muddier than you had pictured it. But the music came loudly as though the quartet were playing on the other bank:

> 'Can there be any day but this
> Though many suns to shine endeavour?'

You sat down, lay down on the bank below the high-tide mark of the river and gave yourself up to the taut blue sky and the need for a necessary death. Huge thrushes stood there all round you, closing in on you, the spots on their breasts growing larger and larger till they throbbed in and out at you as part of the rhythm of the green ministry round you. The stars sprang about you, clawed down at you. You were at peace at last as you heard the water trickling beside you, the tide coming in to take you and the music leading it on. You had your inner space at last. You were being drawn gently from exile to the Kingdom.

You got out a bottle of nembutal capsules that the doctor had given you for when you couldn't sleep and put the contents into your mouth and rolled over to the muddy water and supped up great mouthfuls feverishly whispering: 'Come my beauties. Come my lovely ones.' Then you lay back on the muddy bank and waited for the tide to come and take you.

In a minute your feet and fingers began to tingle. Your feet felt huge. Your thumbs embraced the whole world. They were everything there was. You lay there lulled by the water moving slowly in and out of the rushes beside you. You gazed up at the night sky, the bursting stars, the calling trees, the sharp crescent moon:

> 'At evening hour of calm and peace
> Was Adam's fall made manifest.
> At evening home returned the dove,
> And bore the olive leaf as token.'

The water was reaching your right cheek. You felt it creeping up your right trouser leg. 'At evening hour of calm and peace . . .' But it was daylight again and the sun was burning through your eyelids and your mouth was dry. You woke and found that the tide had gone and left you. You tried to raise your head into the milky white staring sky. It fell back into the mud. Rain was falling on you. Then it was night again and the stars were sharp and there were two crescent moons with faltering inner edges.

The water was touching your right leg and your right arm again. There was water in your ear. You were wet and shivering and you could feel hot urine running down your legs. You tried to lift your head again and sit up. Mud splashed over your face and hair. You heard a voice calling faintly 'Help! Help!' as the water drew near again. You saw some dancers in a group on the dark bank. The voice called out to them. It was the quartet dancing there and playing Mozart. There were four of them. You tried to raise your head and cry out to them but as soon as the voice came they were still. They immediately turned to wooden poles with roughly made masks for faces, and noses and mouths made of chunks of wood roughly tacked on and staring through you, glazed and immobile. 'Oh that this too too solid flesh would melt.' But it remained there stuck in the mud. You could hear the wash of the wind in the trees, and the blood circulating like a main road behind your ears. You could feel your legs tingling and coming back to life. The quartet was playing and dancing again. You tried to call out to them again but your tongue was heavy and your lips thick and dry. You begged them for water but when the voice cried out, they turned to wood again and their eyes and noses dropped off. You turned your face into the water and drank and choked and drank. Weed caught in your teeth and throat. And the tide was rising. The tide was rising to take you, but it only came so far, lapping against you, lifting one hand gently and tenderly dropping it. 'Before the morning watch, I say. Before the morning watch . . .' Then it receded and daylight came and a hard flat white sky. Nothing was waiting to take you.

You tried to get up but your feet had long iron skis attached to them which pushed you sideways and down. It was raining. The trees rattled it down. The birds screamed. You found you could sit up. You got on to one long ski and fell forward against some barbed wire that ran down to the water's edge and into the water. It caught hold of your cheek. You grasped its barbs and clung there up to your waist in water. Your wedding ring hung there on its spikes jangling in the wind. You clung with bleeding hands half-in and half-out of the water. Your head was dragged forward against the barbed wire. It tore your eyelids. 'Help!' You could see a procession coming along the river path, a row of nuns chanting and carrying a rickety wobbling altar behind a priest in festival silver vestments. On the altar stood the Virgin Mary with a simpering smile. She swayed backwards and forwards as they chanted the May morning tune. 'Help!' She winked at you conspiratorially. And behind the nuns came a hearse. They were dragging it along: 'Edward Rutt. Our horses go any distance.' Huge black pompoms wobbled on the horses' heads, and inside were you and your father, you dressed up in white as a child bride with a wreath of syringea around your hair, holding your father's hand, led by your father, Abraham leading Isaac to sacrifice while the nuns sang 'Salva festa dies.' No, you cried and tried to haul yourself along the barbed wire and out of the water. The nuns turned the bend and disappeared. A pad of steaming cow dung was all that was left of the procession, and the marks of tractor wheels running through the dung.

'No' you cried, hauling yourself along the barbed wire trying to reach the bank. And then you were in a plantation of tall spiked sugar canes fighting off two identical boars in identical tartan jackets that plunged at you through the sharp rough canes.

187

'Rupert, come out of there!' you heard a voice. 'Yes, she altered her tweed coat and a cat adopted her . . . They ought to have better crash-barriers. Rupert come out of there!' Then they came up to you, two identical women in the same green skirts and red macintoshes followed by two men in brown with identical shooting sticks.

'Are you all right?' they took you by the armpits and dragged you out of the sugar canes. 'And his shoes!' the identical women were picking up four shoes and helping you across the path and sitting you under a tree. 'These must be your shoes' they put them beside you. 'We wondered what our dog was after. Good thing we came along just then. Is there anything we can do for you?' You shook your head. They walked away only this time upside down, walking against the grey wet sky with their two identical dogs beside them. 'Not much we can do, poor chap. No good giving money, he would probably only drink it. Unemployment, it's a terrible problem, and so much drunkenness goes with it . . .'

. . . 'It was the humidity that helped the ball to swing.'

You sat leaning against a tree with your four shoes. Night came and you tried to stand up but your body was too heavy; your head had a great weight on it and you could feel the shape of your liver. You stood on the path but you fell sideways. You struggled along the path. You tripped against a piece of undigested rock and sat there in the middle of the path with your legs splayed out round you.

Hard rain fell. Chestnut flowers dropped on you, dropped one by one on the path, decayed teeth falling brown on the hard path where you had come with your father. But he had gone and the river denied any knowledge. The rain fell heavily. The wind rose. Twigs burst from the trees. A desolate wind came from the beach road tearing the leaves. You could hear it tugging against the barbed wire and making your wedding ring tinkle and hiss. And the dancers were there again. But when you called out to them sand poured from their mouths. Their faces began slowly disintegrating, trickling away, first nose, then mouth and eyes running out, then their arms in small piles on the ground.

A black hole appeared in the sky and more water poured

188

through it. You dragged yourself back to the shelter of the tree. The sharp yellow swords of blackbirds were piercing the wet earth round you. Two blackbirds face to face over you, holding a worm between them like a skipping rope, letting it swing loose then tugging it taut, letting it drop on your waterlogged legs then plucking it back, straightening it between them. Giant toadstools stood above you, the dark ribbed vaults of their undersides disintegrating on to you. The purple flowers of the lilac were sickening at their tips. You felt hot urine in your pants again and tried to move away from it and wipe the thick grey mud and weed off your clothes and out of your mouth. The river had come again. You could hear its mud greedily supping up the rain. You tried to get up again. The wind banged in your face. A straight track was in front of you. You took a few steps then the rock in it reared up at you. You fell among cow-parsley, its wet showering your face and neck. The wind was blowing the blossoms off the hawthorn and leaving bared shining walls of spikes leaning at you. The wind blew again and made the barbed wire hiss and spit. You could hear the tinkling of your wedding ring again, and the wind coming off the beach road, licking the shingle and turning it to parched bare white bones and the sky a great wound above you dropping down its white pus while the beach boys sang:

'Oh Master when my end is come.'

You fell asleep again and dreamed that Thelma had put up glass doors to control the cow-parsley. Her shadow was behind one of the doors and on it was marked 'Music Limited. Please knock and walk in.'

You woke and lay among the dripping cow-parsley. The rain had waterlogged your clothes. A bird dropped shit in your eyes and you could see only the wild clawing thornbushes advancing their spears. You could hear a sound like toothbrushes working. Slugs were grinding their way over your face.

You got up and found you could walk. You walked then stopped, legs apart, water dripping from your armpits and crotch. You walked again and stopped, walked and stopped.

189

You could see the little platform of the railway halt on its stilt legs miles away. You reached it after about two hours, dragging yourself along the sides of the hedges and supporting yourself up the railway approach by clasping its wooden palings. You had bought a single ticket to get down here. You felt in your pocket for money. But all you pulled out was a wet pulp which you scooped out from your pocket in morsels. You sat down on a bench. You waited for a train. In the evening one came. In your compartment a woman in a flowered dress was explaining to her friend how she got her soufflés into the oven. The green leaves of her dress were parting. The lips of the flowers leaped towards your lips — orchids, their long black genitalia stretching out towards you. There was a necklace of pale intestines hanging round her friend's neck. The buffet-car waiter came down the train carrying a silver platter loaded with human brains stuck with sharp pieces of bone. The woman talking about cookery was sitting against a rock full of fossil worms, beetles, insects, millions of them embedded in the cliff of the British Rail upholstery behind her bare arms. They were climbing out of the soft rock and swarming over her. One crawled on to her mouth as she said 'And I always use a baking tray.'

You picked up a newspaper and tried to read. But the words began to crawl slowly out of the pages at you, the letters that composed them each a plant with a root growing out of the white page, growing, and waiting to grow right off the page, black and swaying and wriggling and reaching out at you taller and taller till the letters' shadows fell over you and you were down on the ground again under the oozing, uttering green.

'And I told her if she wanted her clothes back she'd have to earn them' the people in the compartment were talking.

'. . . Told me they didn't give second mortgages, and I wanted to shake her silly head and ask her if she knew who I was.'

You looked at the newspaper again. The curious plants reared up again at you, shadowing you like giant toadstools, folding down over you to encapsule you. The May morning tune came again. The wound opened again, and you were in that tender room, through the gateway of straining, pressing chestnuts and down at the river, the tide rising, the blossoms falling on the bride. But the music coming didn't call you to the river. You were not the sacrificial son. It came clearly, the tune, but not from there. You felt only horror and disgust at the rearing up of nature and its mounting surge. You waited for the newspaper and the British Rail upholstery and the woman's flowered dress to fall back into their places, for the world to have edges and boundaries again. For May's burst artery to be stemmed, her blood to be congealed. You were cheered by the jogging sound of the train as it carried you back to London. But John Wersby had died.

CHAPTER XIV

You found your front-door key covered in mud and softly unlocked the door of the flat. Julius was still there with Thelma. You could hear them laughing.

'. . . went to this Pak doctor' Thelma was saying, 'because he thought his left eye lacked lustre.'

'. . . dreamed that the Leftists were taking the Rightist road' Julius was saying, 'but it was only his left leg banging against his right one. Chilblains, and he got out of bed to drive the Rightists away and stamped on the concrete floor and fractured his foot.'

Thelma was laughing as she laid the table. You went into the kitchen. There was the sound of lamb chops struggling under the grill. You ran the tap and gulped down cold water. Thelma came in:

'Will! You're back! Oh what a relief! We were so worried. I must ring the police and tell them you're back.' She hugged you. 'You're alive. Julius, Will is back. He's all right. He's alive.' She went into the bathroom and ran you a bath, then she went to the phone. Julius came in.

' "And find my long lost boy" ' he hummed,
' "And bring me to his joy" '.

'Did you find what you were looking for?' he asked.

Thelma was peeling your clothes off and dabbing at the gashes on your face and hands and eyelids. 'But you're back. The tune went? Oh what can we do for you, Will? Ring a doctor?'

'Just leave me alone.'

'Right. Adrian Collins has had to step in and take over the cello for the recital at Cambridge. So you've got no worries there. When did you last eat?'

'Drink.' You gulped down water.

You lay in the bath while Thelma found your pyjamas. Then she banged on the bathroom door: 'Supper's ready.'

She served out lamb chops. You sat at table. Your mouth was dry and your stomach had shrunk after three days without food. It could not hold the food.

Thelma lifted her knife and fork then put them back: 'This meat tastes like dirty washing. It must be horse-meat. I got it down in the East End when I was visiting there this morning.' She sniffed at the meat and pushed her plate away: 'Horse! So now we know how the other half lives.' She tipped the meat into an old shoe-box and Julius put a label on it:

'Horse! Beware!' and put it on the landing for the cleaner to collect with the night's rubbish.

'Horse. Beware' Thelma repeated, 'just in case an old dosser comes along and thinks "Meat ha! My lucky day! One of my meat days." Beware of horse, oh peripatetic stranger. So now we know how the other half lives.'

'Could you both go.'

'Of course. But are you all right alone? And did you find what you were looking for?' Thelma came over and put her arms round you. 'Wide open spaces? Was that what you needed?' You shuddered.

'Wide open spaces!' Julius grimaced. 'Nature's rubbish tip. Man's back yard. What would the face of the earth be like without men? A heap of everything unacceptable. A mass of horn and hoof and stinking cow-parsley.' The thought of cow-parsley made you shudder again. Thelma made you a cup of tea. You shivered at the wastes of nature, the mud and the rain and the sharp rushes and the shingle.

'A mass of damp fungus' Julius went on, 'pushed up like a drowned man floating up to the surface. A scrub of bramble with last year's berries still rotting at its tips. The wide open spaces? Not for me, chum. You can keep the Australian Bush and the Grand Canyon. What news is it to me to meet that great undigested Other? That mindless "I am" before man

193

with infinite propriety took upon himself slowly to clothe its naked ass with the human principle. Glory be to the house and the tower-block. I can't love nature except as an adjunct to cities. Glory be to the tilled fields. The sheep and cattle grazing. A world enclosed from nature. Give me pavements, viaducts, bridges, lock-gates, tunnels and dams.'

'And canals running through the back streets of cities and along the contours of the hills,' Thelma added.

'Man is the membrane. The connective tissue. Just think of the evil stagnating rock underneath us. And the cities built on stilts over it. Cities moored over the rock. Cities tethered there! Extraordinary! I would never think of suicide just because it's all so strange and inventive and perilous and miraculous. Cities and citizens. The only thing the H-Bomb has any use for. Taking out cities. Long live C.N.D. and the human principle.'

'But what about Thorley?' Thelma was saying.

'Oh Thorley is just a garden. A cultivation. An enclosure. And anyway I'm leaving there. I want high-rise cities so much.'

'But the stars' said Thelma, ' and the planets!'

'The stars are just molten gas and the planets are slag-heaps. But you, Will. I've talked too much. What about you? Where are you now?' You drank your tea. 'Adrian Collins likes the John Wersby. I hope you'll come and hear it.' You blocked your ears. 'And we've decided to do the Opus 130 after all.'

'And will Collins go to Australia with you?'

'He'd like to.' There was silence. 'So did you find what you set off to find?' You shook your head.

'I thought you wouldn't. The real call only comes when the answer is already there.'

You waited for them to go. But Julius went on:

'Who would stop to admire the harmony and euphony of the accidentally spilled Scrabble set? The jumble of letters spelling out nothing. Just think of stone. The chaos of stone. Think of it trying to break out under you. Think of all the stone being pushed up every year by the plough, breaking up through the fields, wanting to heave and push down cities.

194

Then stone is tamed by mallet and chisel after millions of years and the Taj Mahal stands there. Nature? No thank you. Give me Regent's Park. Give me Clissold Park. Give me anything but the glories of dark rock and gorging, regurgitating Amazon forest. Give me what man has made. What marvellous things cities are! Delicate fragile structures like balloons moored by one silver thread, man. Constructs are the only beautiful things. Everything else has the quality of the drain. No tension. Nothing urgent. Nothing held back or delayed. Without art just a frightful slackness.'

'Will is tired' Thelma put a bottle in your bed, ' and you are talking too much.'

'Sorry.'

But you felt calmer as Julius talked. You pictured the deserts of Central Asia. The Grand Canyon. The Rockies. The Alps. Nature was the realm of necessity and slackness and death. Art was its interruption. Its arrest.

Julius stood by the table wiping his fingers on some cheese, then nibbling at it. 'I suppose I play to impose a tension over the mindless. Play to control the splaying out of rock and ice and forest. The conquest of the angry, vengeful Gods. And mortality and the wide, loose, open womb of nature.'

'I've been in the river' you said slowly. 'But the tide didn't come and I'm still waiting for it.' And yet your dryness had gone.

'Life is too accidental, Will. Too strange, too chancy, too might-not-have-been to die before one's time.' Thelma and Julius were holding hands.

'Is there anything we can do? Ring a doctor?'

'Go and be happy' you replied. They were still holding hands.

'But what about the children?'

'We'll have to talk about them.'

'Well, we'll be off then' Thelma kissed you. 'I know you want to be on your own.'

'Go and become real' you kissed her. 'We've never given each other a licence to do more than merely exist. We can only diminish each other. We both need a decent space round us.'

She kissed you again and they went and you were relieved.

You sat in your pyjamas and dressing-gown. You went and sat on your bed and scraped mud from under your toenails and hacked at them with scissors and let their hard yellow blades click and snap and fall to the floor. You felt them sharp under your bare feet and hard, like talons, cows' horns, rhinoceros tusks, all the hardness of rock issuing from your soft skin.

You cleaned your fingernails, felt them growing heavily off you into horns, into deer's antlers growing huge out of your fingertips, massive and branching heavily further and further and pushing round their bone soft velvet full of nourishing blood vessels that the birds came down and perched on and ate off till they had picked the last ragged, hanging, swinging rich blood vessels off the rigid antler fingers you had once played music with.

You sat there staring at your immobility, watching helplessly as the birds swung picking at their ends, tearing at the rich velvet that the wind blew at and swung in and out between your antler fingers in long, ragged threads. You stared at your rigid, branching hands impassively, and thought of hands holding a tin-opener and using it, hands holding up sherry glasses at parties and talking about who was going to be next Home Secretary. Or hands on the assembly line adjusting tiny screws on each transistor set as it passes along the belt. And now the fingers were making a cello, fixing its bridge and tightening its strings till they were stretched and taut into a taut blue Mediterranean sky. And the fingers were plucking at them and responding with deep detonations to the violin's high cries of celebration.

But your hands were still the deer's antlers and you sat there watching the birds come down to feed off your ragged velvet strands. You got dressed and rushed down into the churchyard gardens beside Bude Mansions with your stiff, branching bone fingers.

A middle-aged woman and her mother were sitting on the same bench as you each chewing a cheese roll.

'Too cheesy for me' the mother was saying, passing her roll

over to her daughter, and hands came out and unthreaded gratings of cheese from one roll and hands pushed them into the other, and the hands went up to the mouths again and hard teeth came down out of the moist soft gardens of the pink gums and chewed. Then hands were flicking a cigarette lighter on and the daughter had put two cigarettes into her mouth and lit them and passed one to her mother and they puffed and smoked as they had before:

'. . . used to be a dresser up at the Empire. You had to have nimble fingers in those days when it was all quick-fire variety. Now it's the strippers and they don't need her nippy fingers any more.'

Everything was hands moving round you, fingers weaving and unweaving webs of soft and hard things. How strange it was on this slag heap. Hands evolved for tearing meat.

You sat on in the churchyard. A man wove his way on a bicycle through the traffic of the street beyond, jerking on the flexible keys of his fingers with subtle innuendos as he threaded his way past buses and lorries, perilously extended on his fragile, airy steel frame, hands and feet dancing adjustments to the pressures of the street. Hands in the hospital windows held up retorts and poured water into them sucked from huge pipes that leisured under the city. Men wrapped in red blankets sat on the hospital verandah shifting their hands and opening their newspapers. Winds pressed gently like warm hands' palms touching the buildings all round you. Traffic moved and stopped. Birdsong arched over it creating a dome of silence above the city roar. From the cobbled court-yard of the hospital, patients in red blankets were being wheeled across the zebra-crossing to the X-Ray department. The tailor's shop opposite had a shabby grey headless dummy in its window, wearing a tacked-on suit and hands adjusted it. Then there was the little Welsh dairy with its old milk-float standing outside. And the Indian restaurant where a waitress with dirty mascara and dandruff hanging off her eyelashes stood in the doorway shaking a bundle of saffron-stained tablecloths. But your hand were still antlers.

The voices of the people in the gardens came to you:

'. . . said she'd only got half a tight . . .'

' "You're not driving round Australia now so let's have it good," I said to her.'

'. . . Two small Put-U-Ups. It was a lovely way to go.'

'There's mould on this penny.'

'Penicillin.'

'A pen by any other name would smell as sweet.'

'Now don't start getting all philosophical.'

A young dosser with a raw grated face and naked eyes sat down on the bench beside you: 'Got a fag to spare?'

'Sorry' you said.

'Your fingers are all nicotined, so you do smoke.'

'But I'm on a ration. Only two left for today.'

'One each.'

You opened your packet. Your hands were your own again. The birds flew off. 'I'll give you one if you tell me something.'

'And what is it you want to know?'

'Anything. Just anything.'

The young dosser shrugged. 'There used to be all these places. Clean beds for men. St Bryony's House. And the hostels. They was all right. But they've all come down now. Hotels instead. And offices.'

'So where will you sleep tonight?'

He held out his hand. 'You tell me. Hopetown Street?' You gave him the money. Your hands were your hands again. The feeding, pulsing birds had gone. The crackling of their beaks on the blood rich velvet. The grinding of slugs over your face. The stench of damp cow-parsley and the reek of the receding river.

You gave the dosser money and he went away. The conversation from the benches came again:

'. . . Streaky bacon and onions. Real nice mushy onions.'

'. . . and four beautiful roses she painted in twenty minutes and all with a knife . . .'

'. . . lost her putty-coloured drawers up at the hospital.'

'. . . went to Lourdes and got killed by a taxi . . . '

The man in the tailor's shop opposite moved shadowly round his dummy fingering it. A fat bus purred sleekly past. The waitress outside the Indian restaurant still stood there shaking out her saffron-stained tablecloths ... a city pinioned there by fragile but miraculously renewable threads. You wriggled your fingers backwards and forwards. How strange it was on the slag heap.

'Long live C.N.D. and the human principle' you heard Julius say.

You would wait patiently. Perhaps Thelma's departure would give you back a space round you in which you could breathe, or a new liquid in which you could swim.

Or you would wait secretly and without attention for the waters to creep up on you from behind, unexpectedly, when you had given up waiting for them, or when your back was turned, gratuitously, unearned, through no virtue of your own.

Or you would go underground where sleek oil seeped into black basins slowly and secretly inside the arched fortresses of impermeable rock.

Or someone much better than you would take over where you had left off, someone who could assimilate the world of Vietnams and electronic, computerised warfare and nuclear accidents.

Or your body would extend again through some grave dissatisfaction with matter, through brain and shoulder and arms into the fingers' twitching, multiplying movements. And the cello's various, variegated labile cries of a received good would come to you again.

The birds were singing. The pregnant green of May burst out at you again, the plane trees gushing out into geysers of green, the green waterfalling in thick plaited wealth down the grey walls of the churchyard gardens. Perhaps your music would come back as a form of grace that would burst the grey of the city as May green did, an explosive green springing out of the bricks and mortar and dry parched soil and the vats of aspirin that you had been swallowed by.

But as you gazed at the chestnuts throbbing round you heavily, the John Wersby tune came again, winding dangerously subversive out of its Bach-like chorale, interrupting its balm, turning its promise inside out with its own divergent beckoning call:

'Is it very deep?' you had asked your father standing by the river when the big children had gone to school. And he had nodded:

'Very.'

'Suppose that I stood on mother's head, would I be able to reach the top and breathe or would I be deaded?'

'You would still drown.'

And then he had gone down to the river calling after him for you and had never come back, and your mother was standing there by the window of the flat in Maisky Street after the bombing of Guernica saying:

'If ever there were another war . . .'

And you raced down Maisky Street and into the street market and past the stalls loaded with grey furry tripe and soft melts and brown knitted chitterlings spelling out war under the naphtha night flares eating into the fog. And the Korn King was standing there in his Union Jack top hat handing round his black velvet box with the corns and calluses laid out shinily inside in the dark. And the Korn King's top hat had fallen on the ground and he lay there beside it splashing blood on your shoe, and you ran home past 'John Crank, Family and Dispensing Chemist, Mouth Wash Mixtures, Tombs Eureka Indigestion Powders' and 'Edward Rutt, Undertaker, Inexpensive Funerals, Our Horses Go Any Distance' and 'E. West, Family Draper, Inexpensive Mournings a Speciality'.

And you raced home thinking of the Great War and the women in black standing outside the frosted glass saloon bar of The Horns waiting for the lads who would never come home, and the blue night trams rocking past the end of the road in the fog, whining on their two notes: 'Put out your dead'. And your mother's words drummed in your ears:

'If there were ever another war . . .'

'What would we do?' You turned the gas-taps up. But she only pressed her lips together secretively and went on sticking plasticine eyes into the head of the Guy Fawkes she had knitted and which you were going to burn that night.

'Would we do what father did?' But she only said:

'Father died of food poisoning, Will.'

And you stood at the window hearing the pumping creak of invalid carriages and seeing the one-armed man at the tram-points stamping up and down in the freezing air, swinging his real arm round his chest and letting his metal arm clink against the metal rods of the points. And you thought of the zeppelins' secret night creepings over the city and the sinking of the *Lusitania* and the blind men at the corners on crutches with cards round their necks:

'I am a disabled officer.'

'If ever there were another war . . .'

And you had run into the kitchen and looked at the Ideal Boiler:

'Ideal but too small.'

And you did not forget the gas-taps and the Ideal Boiler and the bathchairs pumping up and down the street till the winter of 1940 when you came out of the shelter in the mornings with the smell of damp plaster and dust and rotting joists and charred timbers and singed smoking mattresses in the freezing morning air, and you had snatched at music greedily as an unexpected guest, unaccountable, a received good that nothing could destroy. And your mother was puzzled and worried by the hard, insensitive, fearless child she had produced.

The May morning tune had come again and your father was standing by the water, only he and your mother were no longer the Great War. The filiocides. Abraham leading his son, Isaac, to sacrifice. The tune brought you only a haunting but primitive and irreducible sense of early loss and separation and exile, turning you away from the beach road towards Wappenden and Happenden.

'There are places in the heart which do not yet exist and into them we must enter suffering in order that they may have their existence . . .' Perhaps you would play to give them existence, getting out your cello and bringing your shoulder down heavily on to your bow and sinking the bow deeply into your strings, burning through their fuses to an inner combustion and a coda to the Wersby tune:

'My fleshed leaves will thin.
My rose leaves click and rot.
My son's doom-way
Will be thy bride's unsealing.
Go to thy jewels, Prince.
They are apart.'

You went back to your flat. The door-bell went. George, the first violin, stood there.

'Life is too serious for that, Will' he said as he looked at the gashes in your cheeks and eyelids. 'How art thou?' he kissed you. 'There's a time for mourning and a time to return to the living.'

He was a good pianist and he flipped through your Beethoven Cello and Piano Sonatas and began to play:

'Join me' he cried. You hesitated. You shook your head. 'That's a lovely line. Like a wind coming from far off and promising something loving and tender ... More lovingly there. More tenderly. Aerial gifts. But the cello is replying with a nostalgic wince, a wry "If it were so". He is searching for the lost land with a wry grimace: "If it were so." He is searching for the places he will never reach but which he must continue to search for, yearning. And he throws them away when they come, the promises, the hopes, the suggestions, and just says "Maybe. Perhaps. It will do. It will have to suffice." Get out your cello, Will. It's all so unaccountable. Coming from nowhere and going only to its own ordered ends.'

And as you stood there you remembered how once as a child you had been painting and you had quite deliberately knocked a jar of red paint over the kitchen table and on to the floor and watched the red pool blaze and spread out in different directions, wondering whether it would reach the gas-cooker and the wall, gazing fascinated at what you had done, and seeing how many different directions it would flow into.

'Why did you do that?' your mother had asked staring at the scarlet flower bursting and breaking in every direction

202

over the lino. It was an accident, she had decided, but you had done it as play, simply to see the miraculous bloom rearing out till it became a huge billowing poppy . . . Just to see how it would take itself. Just to see how it would spread. 'Let it last. Let it last' you had cried to yourself as you stared at it. Just to see what could be done with this great scarlet poppy, waiting till it became a field of poppies waving in a gentle wind, opium poppies that would give you vivid dreams. 'Let it never stop' you cried to yourself, picking up your bow. 'Art is always partly play' George sang as he played, and the field of scarlet poppies swayed and bloomed in your mind.